NATIONS HAVE THE RIGHT TO KILL

Also by Richard A. Koenigsberg

Hitler's Ideology: Embodied Metaphor, Fantasy and History

The Nation: A Study in Ideology and Fantasy

The Fantasy of Oneness and the Struggle to Separate:
Towards a Psychology of Culture

NATIONS HAVE THE RIGHT TO KILL

Hitler, The Holocaust and War

Richard A. Koenigsberg

Library of Social Science

Published by Library of Social Science
New York, NY

ISBN 978-0-915042-24-1

Manufactured in the United States of America.

Library of Congress Cataloging-in-Publication Data

Koenigsberg, Richard A.
    Nations have the right to kill : Hitler, the Holocaust, and
war / Richard A. Koenigsberg.
        p. cm.
    Includes bibliographical references.
    ISBN 978-0-915042-24-1 (pbk.)
    1. War--Causes. 2. Politics and war. 3. Genocide. 4. Nationalism--
Psychological aspects. 5. Holocaust, Jewish (1939-1945) 6. World War,
1914-1918--Germany. I. Title.
    JZ6385.K63 2009
    355.02--dc22

For Mei Ha Chan and Orion Anderson, without whom this book could not have been possible.

CONTENTS

PART ONE: THE HOLOCAUST

PART TWO: WAR

PART THREE: THE LOGIC OF WAR AND GENOCIDE

INTRODUCTION

Over 200 million people were killed in the Twentieth Century as a result of acts of violence generated by nation-states and other societal groups. Historians document what occurred, but do we really understand why these things happened. This book—based on forty years of research—contains my findings on the sources and meanings of collective forms of violence.

Scholars study political conflicts as if each one were a discrete case, seeking to identify "causes." But is it possible that there is a fundamental dynamic that leads nations to go to war: an underlying principle that is independent of specific political situations?

I began my research studying Hitler, Nazism and the genocide of the Jews. The Final Solution or Holocaust is a particularly fruitful case study because there was no apparent reason why the Jews had to be killed. Political scientists who rely on "rational choice" theory to explain political events find little in this approach to help them understand the Holocaust.

In 1933, there were only 550,000 Jews in Germany out of a population of 66 million, far less than 1% of the country's population. Jews constituted no threat to Germany. Yet Nazi leaders such as Hitler, Goebbels and Himmler imagined that Jews were acting to destroy their nation—and Western civilization. Why did Hitler and the Nazis believe that this was the case? This book poses and seeks to answer this question.

Nazism sometimes is conceived as an ideology of the "superman." What I found, however, is that Nazi ideology revolved around the idea of sacrifice. According to Hitler, the greatest form of virtue was the willingness of individuals to give their lives over to the community. Jews on the other hand were conceived or imagined by Hitler as people unwilling to sacrifice their lives for a national community.

As I attempted to uncover the roots of the Holocaust, it became evident that the formative experience of Hitler's life was his participation in the First World War. My research moved toward examining this other instance of societal mass slaughter. This book reports the results of my odyssey, focusing on my discovery of a similar psychological dynamic at the root of both the First World War and the Holocaust.

Like Nazism, ideologies that gave rise to the First World War revolved around the idea of sacrifice, which is intimately linked to the ideology of nationalism. During the First World War, millions of young men were sent into battle, killed and wounded in the name of entities given names like France, Great Britain, Russia and Germany.

The ideology of national self-sacrifice led to monumentally destructive results. Approximately 6,000 men died per day in the course of the war—that began in 1914 and ended in 1918. In spite of perpetual slaughter, the war persisted. The scope of destruction brought about by the First World War—9 million dead and nearly 21 wounded—seems incomprehensible.

This book seeks to decipher the meaning of the massive destruction that occurred during the First World War—and to link what happened in this war with what occurred during the Holocaust and Second World War. I attempt to demonstrate that in each case, political violence was generated according to the dynamic of sacrifice. Is it possible that human beings can be possessed by this sort of "madness"—a willingness to sacrifice millions of human beings in the name of abstract entities called nations? I present evidence showing that this was the case.

The magnitude of political violence and destruction that occurred during the Twentieth Century is difficult to fathom. We are capable of knowing what occurred—the facts are part of the historical record and beyond doubt—but we tend to conceive of events as if they emanate from a domain of reality separate from human motivation. It is difficult to conceive that we human beings are the source of what occurred; that we willed these events into being.

Adolf Hitler is the central focus of my study. This single individual played a profound role in the history of the Twentieth Century. Some people claim that Hitler was an anomaly. What I document in this book, however, is that Hitler's thinking was firmly rooted in the central ideologies of the Twentieth Century. Hitler embraced the very ordinary ideologies of nationalism, racism and warfare—and carried them to an extreme, bizarre conclusion.

Hitler's actions, I believe, convey something that is important for us to understand. Hitler participated in the First World War, witnessed the endless carnage, experienced the horror of warfare, but was unable to abandon it. He refused to complain about the deaths of 2 million German soldiers because—"After all, were they not dying for Germany?" (*Mein Kampf*, 1962)

Hitler did approach performing a critique of warfare when he posed the question (in *Mein Kampf*, 1962): "Why do some men die in battle—sacrifice their lives—whereas other men do not?" This question quickly transformed itself, however, into a condemnation of Jews: Why, Hitler asked, had German men died in the First World War, whereas Jewish (German) men had not?

Although there was no evidence to support Hitler's claim, nevertheless he believed that Jews had been "shirkers" during the First World War: had avoided participating in battle. Hitler became obsessed with the idea that Jews had acted to escape the sacrificial obligation. This belief became the basis for his anti-Semitism. Hitler conceived or imagined Jews as people who were unwilling to sacrifice themselves for a national community.

As soon as Hitler took power in 1933 and became Chancellor of Germany, he began fantasizing about a Second World War. He did not shrink from the idea of repeating the sacrifice of German soldiers that had occurred during the First World War. When he declared war on September 1, 1939, he asked every German to be prepared to do what he was willing to do (and eventually did): to lay down their lives for their country.

But if Germans were going to die in the Second World War, what about Jews? If Hitler had the "right" to require that his soldiers be obedient unto death, why should Jews be allowed to live? These reflections led Hitler to an "insight" that provided the rationale for the Final Solution.

As the Holocaust began, Hitler professed to be undisturbed by the murder of men, women and children. "If I don't mind sending the pick of the German people into the hell of war without regret for the spilling of precious German blood," Hitler declared, "then I have naturally the right to destroy millions of men of inferior races who increase like vermin" (Meltzer, 1976). If Hitler had the right to ask his own soldiers—the best people—to die, why did he not also have the right to send Jews—the worst people and mortal enemies of the German people—to their deaths?

As German soldiers were being slaughtered, so Jews would be slaughtered. The Final Solution represented an enactment—created by Hitler and the Nazis—conveying the abject condition of a human being that has been required to give his body over to the nation-state. German soldiers had been conceived as masculine warriors or heroes. But on the Eastern Front in the Soviet Union they were like Jews in the death camps—pathetic and abject—freezing, starving and dying in prodigious numbers in places like Stalingrad.

Although historians write about the desire for conquest, economic gain and many other factors that motivate societies to go to war, one product of warfare remains constant: death, maiming, and the destruction of the artifacts of civilization. We view death, maiming and the destruction of the artifacts of civilization, however, as by-products: things that occur as nations and leaders pursue other objectives.

But what if destruction and self-destruction are the fundamental purpose of warfare? This is the conclusion that I have reached. More precisely, perhaps warfare is undertaken as a form of sacrifice—a gigantic potlatch—whereby human beings give over their bodies and possessions to objects of worship with names like France, Germany, Japan, America, etc.

We would prefer not to know that this is the case. We still exist within the heart of the storm. Nationalism is a living religion, so powerful that we barely conceive of it as a religion. Yet Carolyn Marvin in her ground-breaking *Blood Sacrifice and the Nation* (1999) develops a theory similar to the one I present in this book. She shows how warfare and sacrifice function to support and sustain the idea of the nation.

I explore this idea in Chapter III of this book, "As the Soldier Dies, So the Nation Comes Alive," as well as in Chapter V, in which I examine parallels between the First World War and the Aztec performance of warfare as a ritual sacrifice. Are we in the Western World similar to the Aztecs in that we sacrifice human beings in the name of our Gods?

Sadly, it would appear that this is the case. The difference is that the Aztecs were aware that warfare was a sacrificial ritual, whereas we in the West are not yet aware of this. One objective of this book is to help us to become conscious of the central role of sacrifice in our political rituals.

Marvin writes about blood sacrifice in war as the "totem secret." The fact that nations create warfare as a sacrificial ritual is something that we are not supposed to know. Indeed, we don't wish to know that this is the case. What would it mean if people were to become aware that warfare is an institution whose purpose is to sacrifice—or kill—people?

Hitler nearly understood this. He realized that nations have the right to kill. The purpose of this book is to provide documentation showing how nations act in the name of killing or sacrificing people.

We understand that nations have the right to kill, but assume there are specific reasons why states find it necessary to go to war.

But what if it turns out that the production of sacrificial violence and victims is an essential function of the nation-state? What if wars are waged not for specific reasons, rather in order to produce opportunities for killing and dying? What if it turns out that killing (producing sacrificial victims) is one of the fundamental purposes of collective acts of violence? If we become capable of knowing this, will it make a difference?

PART ONE

THE HOLOCAUST

CHAPTER I

The Logic of the Holocaust

INTRODUCTION

By delineating the mindset of Hitler and the Nazis, it is possible to reveal the logic that was the source of the Holocaust. We begin by conceptualizing the Final Solution as a collective project that was consciously undertaken by and profoundly significant to many people. To understand the Holocaust, therefore, is to reveal the meaning of the project that Hitler conceived and put into action. The question of motivation grows out of the issue of meaning. What was the purpose of mass murder? What did Hitler believe he would accomplish by exterminating the Jews? What did Hitler and the Nazis aspire to achieve through the Final Solution?

I conclude that the Final Solution grew out of a coherent structure of thought. In *Hitler's Ideology* (Koenigsberg, 1975) I analyzed the central metaphors in Hitler's writings and speeches. Hitler's perception of reality grew out of a coherent fantasy. This fantasy supported and sustained the ideology that dictated action on the stage of history.

JEWISH DISEASE WITHIN THE
GERMAN BODY POLITIC

At the core of Hitler's ideology lay his conception of the German nation as an actual body politic imagined to be under attack. The life of this organism was threatened by Jewish bacteria—whose continued presence within the nation would lead to the death of Germany. Hitler described the Jew typically as the "demon of the disintegration of peoples, symbol of the unceasing destruction of their lives." [1] In order to rescue Germany—to save the life of the body politic—it was necessary to eliminate from within the nation those forces that threatened to destroy it. Genocide grew out of Hitler's conviction that in order to prevent the death of Germany, it was necessary to exterminate the Jewish people.

Hitler's project was to rescue his nation—to "prevent our Germany from suffering, as Another did, the death upon the Cross." Hitler believed that his project was the most significant one that a human being could undertake. In the name of rescuing Germany, everything was deemed permissible:

> We may be inhumane, but if we rescue Germany we
> have achieved the greatest deed in the world. We may
> work injustice, but if we rescue Germany then we have
> removed the greatest injustice in the world. We may
> be immoral, but if our people is rescued we have once
> more opened the way for morality.

Hitler stated that the purpose of National Socialism was to "maintain the life of Germany." He conceived of Germany as a living organism with the German people constituting "cells" of this organism. Jews constituted pathogenic cells (bacteria or viruses) whose continued presence within the national body would lead to disease and death. In

---

1 Unless otherwise noted, citations of Hitler are taken from Baynes (1942), *The Speeches of Adolf Hitler* and De Roussy de Sales (1941), *My New Order*.

Mein Kampf (1962), Hitler stated that Germans would choose as their leader someone who "profoundly recognizes the distress of his people" and who, after he has attained "the ultimate clarity" with regard to the nature of the disease "seriously tries to cure it." In Hitler's mind, he was that unique politician who possessed the insight to diagnose Germany's disease, capacity to prescribe a cure, and determination to carry out the necessary treatment.

Hitler posed the question: "Could anyone believe that Germany alone was not subject to exactly the same laws as all other human organisms?" In his diary on March 27, 1942, Goebbels described the process of extermination as "pretty barbaric and not to be described in detail," but overcame his compunctions noting that Germany's actions reflected a "life-and-death struggle between the Aryan race and the Jewish bacillus."

In his 1935-6 propaganda booklet, Himmler observed (Padfield, 1990) that the battle against peoples conducted by Jews had belonged "so far as we can look back, to the natural course of life on our planet." Therefore one could calmly reach the conviction that the struggle of nations against Jews—of life against death—was quite as much a law of nature as "man's struggle against some epidemic; as the struggle of a healthy body to eliminate plague bacillus."

Why did Nazi leaders use these biological metaphors? What did Hitler have in mind when he stated that Germany was subject to the same laws as "all other human organisms?" What was the "law of nature" that led Himmler to conclude that the struggle of nations against Jews represented the struggle of a healthy body against "plague bacillus"? Hitler and Himmler were referring, I believe, to the law of the immune system: that biochemical mechanism or system operating within organisms that works to destroy each and every cell identified as "not self."

Jews in the mind of Hitler represented a foreign microorganism within the bloodstream of Germany. Since Jews were pathogenic micro-organisms within the body politic, it was necessary that they be destroyed. Indeed, each and every one of these Jewish bacteria or viruses had to be removed from the body politic, lest they begin again to divide and multiply. SS-men functioned as if "killer cells" within the German body politic, assigned the task of identifying, tracking down and destroying Jewish micro-organisms.

On the evening of February 22, 1942, Hitler met with Himmler and a Danish SS major and expounded his conviction (Wistrich, 1985) that:

> The discovery of the Jewish virus is one of the greatest revolutions that has taken place in the world. The battle in which we are engaged today is of the same sort as the battle waged, during the last century, by Pasteur and Koch. How many diseases have their origin in the Jewish virus! We shall regain our health only by eliminating the Jew.

Hitler conceived of the Final Solution from the perspective of immunology. As "Doctor of the German people" he would act to save Germany's life by destroying pathogens that were the source of the nation's disease. Nazism revolved around the idea or fantasy that Germany was an actual body whose life was endangered by foreign cells within its bloodstream. The Final Solution represented a systematic effort to remove alien cells from within the body politic, thereby destroying the source of disease and saving the nation's life.

The central fantasy contained within or articulated by Hitler's ideology was that of Germany as an organism containing Jewish bacteria and viruses whose removal was necessary if the nation was to survive. However, what is the meaning of this extraordinary idea? Nations are not bodies and Jews are not bacteria. Why did this metaphor resonate with the German people? Let us approach this question by viewing Nazism as a religion.

DEVOTION TO GERMANY

"Das deutsche Volk, das deutsche Volk, das deutsche Volk" were words echoing throughout Germany in the early Thirties (Holt, 1936). Hitler's religion of Nazism permitted the German people to worship themselves; to bow down to their own nation and nationality. In the United States we say, "I pledge allegiance to the flag of the United States of America and to the republic for which it stands, one nation under God..."

The oath of the SS-man was: "I swear to you, Adolf Hitler, as Fuehrer and Reichschancellor of the German Reich, loyalty and bravery. I swear to you, and to those you have named to command me, obedience unto death, so help us God." Nazism was a pledge of allegiance in its most radical form; the apogee (or nadir) of Western nationalism.

A great deal has been written about the Holocaust from the perspective of "obedience to authority." However, it is misleading to conceptualize Nazi willingness to follow orders as passive acquiescence. Rather, what commentators characterize as obedience was understood and experienced by the Nazis as duty, loyalty, faithfulness and a willingness to sacrifice for the community. This quality of active devotion lay at the heart of the Nazi revolution.

Hitler himself was the greatest devotee of his own religion. He declared, "We do not want to have any other God—only Germany." He inspired others to worship the god that he worshipped, indeed insisted that they do so. Though cynical and devious in his pursuit of power, Hitler's devotion to Germany was sincere and profound. He proclaimed:

> Our future is Germany. Our today is Germany. And our past is Germany. Let us take a vow this morning, at every hour, in each day, to think of Germany, of the nation, of our German people. You cannot be unfaithful to something that has given sense and meaning to your whole existence.

Hitler explained: "Our love towards our people will never falter, and our faith in this Germany of ours is imperishable." He called *Deutschland ueber Alles* a profession of faith, which today "fills millions with a greater strength, with that faith which is mightier than any earthly might." Nationalism for Hitler meant willingness to act with a "boundless, all embracing love for the Volk and, if necessary, to die for it."

Hitler stated that *Volksgemeinschaft* meant "overcoming bourgeois privatism, unconditionally equating the individual fate and the fate of the nation." Every single German was obligated to unite with the community; to embrace and share the common faith. According to Hitler, no one was "excepted from the crisis of the Reich." The Volk, he explained to the German people, is "but yourselves. There may not be a single person who excludes himself from this joint obligation." Hitler's totalitarianism insisted upon absolute identification with the community. Not a single person was exempt from the obligation to devote one's life to Germany and make enormous sacrifices in her name.

Hitler declared: "We are fanatic in our love for our people. We can go as loyally as a dog with those who share our sincerity, but we will pursue with fanatic hatred the man who believes that he can play tricks with this love of ours." Hitler's rage was directed toward people whom he imagined did not share his faith. He experienced these people as mocking his own belief and sincerity:

> Our aim is the dictatorship of the whole people, the community. I began to win men to the idea of an eternal national and social ideal—to subordinate one's own interests to the interest of the whole society. There are, nevertheless, a few incurables who had never understood the happiness of belonging to this great, inspiring community.

Calling people who refused to subordinate personal interests to the interest of society "incurables" suggests that Hitler conceived of those who did not wholeheartedly wish to belong to the community as people suffering from a disease. Those who did not believe in and wish to devote themselves to Hitler, the Nazi movement and the German community were somehow "sick." Thus, the "disease within the body of the people"—to which Hitler so often referred— symbolized disbelief in Nazi ideology or lack of faith. It was precisely the disease of disbelief or lack of faith that Hitler sought to eradicate.

JEWISH INDIVIDUALISM AS NEGATION OF THE GERMAN COMMUNITY

If Nazi ideology was based on profound attachment and devotion to Germany, Jews symbolized the opposite of attachment and devotion to Germany. The metaphor that appeared with greatest frequency in Hitler's speeches as a description of Jews was *Zerzetzung*, translated as "force of disintegration." This German word—widely used in chemistry and biology—means that which breaks things down into their component elements; decomposition, decay, or putrefaction.

This term suggested that the Jewish race worked to destroy all "genuine values." Jews symbolized negation of everything sacred to the German people—their traditions, culture, position in the world, patriotism, and patriotic symbols (Blackburn, 1984). Goebbels declared in January 1945 that Jews were the "incarnation of that destructive drive which in these terrible years rages in the enemies' warfare against everything that we consider noble, beautiful and worth preserving."

Jews symbolized that which called into question the fundamental beliefs and values of the German people. The Aryan was conceived by Hitler as someone willing to sacrifice for the community, while Jews stood for individualism—unwillingness to sacrifice for the community. If the good German was characterized by idealistic devotion to a cause, Jews represented the inability to become devoted to a cause. Goebbels contrasted the "creative, constructive philosophy of National Socialism with its idealistic goals" to the Jewish philosophy of "materialism and individualism." Jews were seen as lacking a soul—the precise opposite of the heroic, self-sacrificing Aryan.

Hitler bluntly told his audiences, "You are nothing, your nation is everything." The fundamental premise of Nazi ideology was that the individual achieved identity only by virtue of his or her relationship to the nation; that the individual found fulfillment only by virtue of subordination to the community. The essence of morality, according to this conception, was willingness to sacrifice personal interest in the name of one's nation.

Hitler's Official Programme published in 1927 (Feder, 1971) put forth as its central plank: "The Common Interest before Self Interest," stating that "The leaders of our public life all worship the same god—Individualism. Personal interest is the sole incentive." Within the framework of National Socialist morality, the fundamental "sins" were individualism and the pursuit of private, personal interests. National Socialism sought to teach or compel people to overcome the sin of individualism.

The psychological dynamic that generated the Holocaust grew out of conflict between the ideal of *Volksgemeinschaft*—the community of the German people—on the one hand, and ideas of individualism or individuality on the other. The fundamental characteristic of Jews according to Nazi ideology was their "free-floating" quality: inability to form an organic tie to a national community. The Jew was compelled by his very nature to pursue private, selfish interests. The Jewish tendency toward individualism, Hitler believed, acted to shatter or "disintegrate" the human being's tie to a national community.

The following judgment by the Cologne Labor Court (January 21, 1941) denied the claim of Jewish employees to a vacation (Noakes & Pridham, 2001):

> The precondition for the claim to a vacation—membership of the plant community—does not exist.

> A Jew cannot be a member of the plant community on
> account of his whole racial tendency, which is geared
> to forwarding his personal interests and securing
> economic advantages.

By virtue of his racially inherited tendency toward "forwarding
personal interests and securing economic advantages," Jews were
imagined to be incapable of participating in the life of a community.
Hitler called Jews the "ferment of decomposition in peoples," which
meant that the Jew "destroys and must destroy." Therefore, Hitler
said, it is "beside the point whether the individual Jew is 'decent'
or not. In himself he carries those characteristics which Nature has
given him."

Hitler stated that the Jew completely lacked the "conception of
an activity which builds up the life of the community." Nazi scholarship declared (Aronsfeld, 1985) that the peculiar characteristic
of Judaism was its "hostility to human society," which is why there
could be "no solution to the Jewish question." A true understanding
of Jews and Judaism "insists on their total annihilation."

The Jewish tendency toward selfish individualism (fixed by he-
redity according to Hitler) meant that they were unable to comprehend the meaning and necessity of national self-sacrifice. The Final
Solution was intended to punish Jews for their anti-social unwillingness to participate in the life of the community; to demonstrate that
sacrifice was required of everyone; and to show Jews (and everyone
else) that it was impossible to escape, evade or resist the embrace
of the nation-state.

WHO SHALL LIVE AND WHO SHALL DIE?

Hitler's ideology was intimately bound to the idea of national
self-sacrifice. Writing about the First World War (in which 2 million German soldiers were killed and over 4 million wounded),
Hitler said: "When in the long war years Death snatched so many

dear comrades and friends from our ranks, it would have seemed to me almost a sin to complain—after all, were they not dying for Germany?" It would appear that Hitler accepted—did not rebel against—the monumental sacrifices that had been made by German soldiers.

Nevertheless, after the war, questions arose in the mind of Hitler and some other Germans. This questioning took the form of reflections upon the following paradox: Why had some people died in the war, whereas others had not? Specifically, why had the best Germans—patriotic young men in the prime of life—been sent indiscriminately to their deaths, while other "inferior" people had not participated in battle, and survived.

This kind of question was the basis for the "euthanasia" movement that began to take hold subsequent to the First World War. In their influential book, *Permission for the Destruction of Life Unworthy of Life* (1920; see Noakes & Pridham, 2001) two eminent German scholars—lawyer Karl Binding and psychiatrist Alfred Hoche—wrote as follows:

> If one thinks of a battlefield covered with thousands of dead youth and contrasts this with our institutions for the feebleminded with their solicitude for their living patients— then one would be deeply shocked by the glaring disjunction between the sacrifice of the most valuable possession of humanity on one side and on the other the greatest care of beings who are not only worthless but even manifest negative value.

On the battlefields of the First World War, the state had squandered the lives of healthy young men. In mental hospitals, on the other hand, the state showed the greatest solicitude and devoted the greatest care toward assuring the survival of human beings who were not only worthless, but who manifest "negative value." If the state was willing to sacrifice the lives of its soldiers, why should so many resources be expended to keep mental patients alive? Why did the state devote so much energy to caring for mental patients while it was so promiscuous with the lives of soldiers?

Based on the logic of ideas like this about life that was unworthy of life, the euthanasia movement gained a foothold—and led to mass-murder when the Nazis took power. In August, 1939, psychiatrists began (with Hitler's authorization) to kill defective or disabled children. In 1939—two years before the beginning of the Final Solution—a program for the killing of adult mental patients was put into practice, leading to the deaths of nearly 100,000 people.

A major figure in the euthanasia movement, Dr. Hermann Pfannmueller, declared (Lifton, 1986) that the idea was unbearable to him that "the best, the flower of our youth must lose its life at the front in order that feeble-minded and irresponsible asocial elements can have a secure existence in the asylum." What was unbearable was that the state had no qualms about sending its most valuable members—healthy, devoted soldiers—to die in war, while it took great pains to preserve the lives of feeble-minded and asocial people who did not contribute to the community.

The killing of mental patients appears to have grown out of the logic that inferior people had to be killed in order to "balance things out." If the state did not hesitate to send its healthiest stock to die in war—vigorous, young men—then surely it should have no compunctions or misgivings about killing the mentally ill—people who were unhealthy and made no contribution to society. Mental patients were one of several classes of people whom the Nazis defined as "parasites on the body of the people"; human beings who consumed national resources, but did not create or produce them.

In *Mein Kampf*, Hitler raised the question—Why do the best die while the worst survive?—in moral terms. The best human beings were those who willingly abandoned personal interests in the name of serving the community. The very best human beings were people like Hitler's comrades in the First World War: those who did not shrink from making the "supreme sacrifice;" who were willing to be obedient unto death and to die for Germany.

According to our ordinary sense of justice, moral virtue is rewarded, while the absence of moral virtue is punished. Hitler observed that in warfare the opposite was the case. Those who were the most virtuous—willing to fight for their country—were punished (with injury or death). Whereas those who lacked moral virtue (e.g., war deserters or shirkers)—unwilling to fight for their country—were rewarded (were not injured and did not lose their lives). If those who were morally virtuous had to surrender their bodies to the nation-state and to die in war, why should others—people who lacked moral virtue—be spared such a fate?

JEWS TOO SHALL DIE

The extermination of the Jews—the Final Solution—began in late 1941 prior to the development of death camps and gas chambers. As the German army waged war and penetrated into the Soviet Union, they were followed closely by the *Einsatzgruppen* or mobile killing units. It is estimated that more than 1.5 million Jews were killed on the Eastern Front.

By the end of the winter of 1941-42, more than 90% of the Jews trapped by the Germans east of the Soviet border had been killed. The extermination of men, women, and children apparently did not disturb Hitler. "If I don't mind sending the pick of the German people into the hell of war without regret for the shedding of valuable German blood," Hitler declared, "Then I have naturally the right to destroy millions of men of inferior races who increase like vermin" (Meltzer, 1976).

The logic of extermination or genocide is contained within this statement. Hitler knew that as commander-in-chief of the army he would not be faulted if he sent young Germans into battle. This was his prerogative as leader of the armed forces. If Hitler had the "right" to send German soldiers to die—had no compunctions or regrets about doing so—why then should he not also have the right—have no compunctions or regrets—about sending Jews to their deaths?

If a national leader is allowed to send its best people—its soldiers—
to die, why would a national leader not also be allowed to send the
worst people—mortal enemies of one's nation—to die?

A sign at the entrance to Auschwitz appeared to mock or taunt
the Jews as they entered the camp: "I bid you welcome. This is not a
holiday resort but a labor camp. Just as our soldiers risk their lives
at the front to gain victory for the Third Reich, you will have to work
here for the welfare of a new Europe" (Hellman, 1981). This message may appear cynical, but it contains logic: "Just as our soldiers
are sacrificing our lives for Germany, so you will be required to die
when Germany asks you to."

The Final Solution was intended by Hitler to convey the following message to Jews—and everyone else: "Do not think anyone
is exempt from the obligation to sacrifice their lives for Germany.
Just as our soldiers are suffering and dying in battle, so you too will
be compelled to suffer and die in the camps." Jews—like German
soldiers—would be required to give over their bodies and souls to
the German nation-state.

The Final Solution came into being in order to teach Jews a lesson
by punishing them for their "selfish individualism." Jews symbolized
the idea that it was possible to evade the German nation-state; to
exist in a condition of separateness from the community. The Final
Solution demonstrated that it was impossible to separate from the
national community; that the nation-state controlled the lives of
each and every human being within its boundaries. The obligation
to submit to the nation—to sacrifice one's life for Germany—could
not be evaded.

The logic of the Holocaust followed from the logic of domination
and sacrificial death that constituted the essence of National Socialism. Hitler's ideology glorified the nation-state at the same time that it
diminished the significance of the individual. Hitler explained to the
German people, "You are nothing, your nation is everything." The nation or national community constituted an "absolute." The individual
attained significance only insofar as he could contribute to the national
community.

On the other hand, Hitler believed that some people were incapable or unwilling to sacrifice for or contribute to a national community. This was the symbolic significance of the term "Jew:" A human being that wished to exist in a condition of separation from the national community and had no desire to contribute to the well-being of this community.

The idea that some people believed they were exempt from the obligation to submit to the national community—sacrifice for Germany—enraged Hitler. Why were some people required to give over their lives—to die for Germany—whereas others were not? Why in the First World War had German soldiers died in massive numbers while Jewish "shirkers" had avoided fighting and dying? Jews symbolized people who believed that it was unnecessary to—possible to avoid—sacrificing for the national community.

Hitler could not bear to contemplate the idea of freedom; to consider the possibility that people are not required to surrender their lives to the nation-state. German soldiers and SS-men had vowed "obedience unto death." Why should some people be allowed to get off "scot free"? In a docudrama on the Wannsee Conference (where on January 20, 1942, high-ranking Nazis and German government leaders gathered for the purpose of discussing the "final solution to the Jewish question in Europe"), a Nazi official argues in favor of the Final Solution by posing the question: "Will the Jews be in luxury in warm concentration camps while our soldiers freeze at the Eastern Front?"

The Final Solution was undertaken in order to demonstrate that no one was exempt from the obligation to suffer and die for Germany. No one would evade the sacrificial obligation. Everyone would be required to submit. If German soldiers were suffering and dying in massive numbers on the field of battle, so Jews would be required to suffer and die in massive numbers in the camps. If the German nation could compel its best people to die, surely it had the right to send the worst people—Jews, enemies of the German people—to their deaths. The logic of genocide was based on the logic of warfare.

Warfare requires that soldiers give over their bodies and souls to the nation-state. They are required to suffer and die when their nation and its leaders ask them to do so. The Holocaust represented an extension of the logic that allows the nation-state to compel people to die. Jews—like German soldiers—were required to give over their bodies and souls to the nation; compelled to die when Germany asked them to do so. The Final Solution enacted the idea of "dying for the country"—stripped of words such as loyalty, honor and duty.

CHAPTER II

The Sacrificial Meaning
of the Holocaust

INTRODUCTION

At the heart of Hitler's ideology is the idea that the capacity for self-sacrifice constitutes the foundation of civilization. Hitler distinguished between those willing to surrender their lives to the community—submit to the nation—and those unwilling to do so. The Aryan or good Nazi represented an individual who was willing to sacrifice unconditionally. Jews, on the other hand, represented people who were unwilling or unable to sacrifice for the community.

Jews were conceived as people intent on tearing down Nazi ideals: selfish individualists who lacked faith in Hitler and Germany and refused to sacrifice in the name of the sacred community. Hitler became enraged when contemplating the idea that some people— like German soldiers in the First World War—were required to sacrifice their lives for the nation, whereas other people seemed to be exempt from this sacrificial obligation.

The essential characteristic of the Jew from Hitler's perspective was his unwillingness or incapacity to renounce individuality in the name of the community. The Final Solution was undertaken in order to demonstrate that no one was exempt from the obligation to submit to the nation-state. Jews too—like German soldiers—would be compelled to die when Hitler asked them to do so.

WORSHIPPING GERMANY

Hitler proclaimed, "We do not want to have any other God, only Germany." Nazism was a form of religion and Hitler a fanatic preacher, obsessed with the idea of Germany, imploring and beseeching others to worship and devote their lives to the god that he worshipped. Hitler explained to his people:

> Our future is Germany. Our today is Germany. And our past is Germany. Let us take a vow this morning, at every hour, in each day, to think of Germany, of the nation, of our German people. You cannot be unfaithful to something that has given sense and meaning to your whole existence.

The foundation of Nazi totalitarianism was the ideal of *Volksgemeinschaft*—the community of the German people. *Volksgemeinschaft*, Hitler said, meant "overcoming bourgeois privatism" in order to "unconditionally equate the individual fate and the fate of the nation." Everyone was required to participate:

> No one is excepted from the crisis of the Reich. This Volk is but yourselves. There may not be a single person who excludes himself from this joint obligation.

Nazi ideology represented a radical form of nationalism affirming *absolute identity* between self and country; insisting that there was no such thing as a sphere of existence *separate* from the life of the national community.

Germany was like a jealous, wrathful god that would brook no opposition. No one was exempt from the obligation to worship and bow down to her. Genocide represented religious war against infidels—"death to the non-believers"—compelling Jews to acknowledge the power of the German god. The Final Solution was undertaken in order to demonstrate that Germany was omnipotent and could not be evaded. Everyone was required to submit, that is, to give over one's body to the nation-state.

Jews symbolized the idea that it was possible to exist separately from the community, thus shattering Hitler's fantasy of an omnipotent community that embraced everyone and contained everything within its boundaries. Hitler characterized the Jew again and again as a "force of disintegration" working to destroy Germany. What did this mean?

JEWISH DESTRUCTIVENESS

The German word *Zerzetzung* is a term used in chemistry meaning the "act or process of simplifying or breaking down a molecule into smaller parts." The word is commonly translated as "decomposing" or "disintegrating" or "causing to decay". When used in relation to the Jews, this term suggested that the Jewish people worked toward the destruction of all "genuine values" and of everything that was sacred to Germans (Blackburn, 1984): their traditions, culture, patriotism, patriotic symbols, etc. Goebbels stated that Jews were the "incarnation of that destructive drive which in these terrible years rages in the enemies' warfare against everything that we consider noble, beautiful and worth preserving."

Nazism evokes violence, cynicism and brutality. The Nazis did not conceive of themselves in these terms. Goebbels stated that to be a socialist meant to "subordinate the I to the Thou, sacrifice the personality for the whole." He defined Socialism as "service, renunciation for individuals and a claim for the whole, fanatic of love, courage to sacrifice, resignation for the Volk." National Socialism, according to Goebbels, was based upon willingness to sacrifice and to abandon individuality in the name of devoting one's self to the community.

Scholars often interpret Nazism according to the concept of "obedience to authority." Germans who followed Hitler did so, however, in a spirit of active devotion rather than passive submission. Rudolph Hess said, "We know nothing but carrying out Hitler's orders—and thus we prove our faith in him." A U.S. Department of State booklet written during the war (Murphy, 1943) explicated Nazi ideology as a force or conviction that "consecrates its whole life to the service of an idea, a faith, a task or a duty even when it knows that the destruction of its own life is certain."

Jews were conceived as people who refused to sacrifice for the sake of a national community. Goebbels claimed that the Jewish philosophy of "materialism and individualism" stood in stark contrast to the creative, constructive philosophy of National Socialism and its idealistic goals. *Hitler's Official Programme*, published in 1927 (Feder, 1971), inveighed against the leaders of public life who all worshipped the same god—"individualism"—and whose sole incentive was "personal interest." The essence of the Nazi's complaint against Jews was that they lacked the capacity for self-sacrifice. By virtue of his unwillingness to surrender to the community, the Jew seemed to mock and spoil German idealism.

WAR AS A SACRIFICIAL RITUAL

Steven Kull (1984) discusses the military ethos, which revolves around the willingness of the individual to sacrifice himself in order to fulfill the abstract purposes of a group:

> The emergence of self-sacrificing behavior in humans represents an extraordinary deviation from previously established patterns. It is awesome that after billions of years of producing life forms that adhere tenaciously

to the goal of survival, evolution suddenly developed
a form that intentionally sacrifices itself in the name
of abstract principles.

Kull hypothesizes that these self-sacrificing behaviors are generated
by the activity of the cortex "overriding the more primitive tenden-
cies of the lower brain."

Gwynne Dyer in his classic study *War* (1985) quotes General
John Hackett: "You offer yourself to be slain: This is the essence of
being a soldier. By becoming soldiers, men agree to die when we tell
them to." Writing about the First World War, Joanna Bourke (1996)
notes that the most important point to be made about the male body
during that war is that it was "intended to be mutilated." In the First
World War, the nations of France, Great Britain and Germany asked
soldiers to get out of trenches and to run toward opposing trenches,
where they frequently were cut down by machine-gun fire and artillery shells. It is estimated that 9 million men were killed and over
21 million wounded in the First World War.

In our conventional way of thinking, we say that when a soldier
dies it is because the enemy killed him. When French Soldiers in the
First World War got out of their trenches and moved into No Man's
Land to encounter artillery shells and machine-gun fire from the opposing side, we say that Germans killed them. Likewise when German
soldiers moved forward *en masse* to be slaughtered by machine-guns
and artillery shells, we say that they were killed by French soldiers.

Wouldn't it be more parsimonious to say that these nations
and their leaders—by putting young men into such untenable situations—killed their own soldiers? One may suggest that during
the First World War, France and its leaders killed French soldiers;
Germany and its leaders killed Germans soldiers; and Great Britain
and its leaders killed British soldiers. Of course, we'd prefer not to
say it this way. We disguise the sacrificial meaning of warfare by
holding the *other nation* responsible for the death of our soldiers.

Yet commentators at the time often did conceptualize this war
from the perspective of sacrifice. Writing in 1916, P. H. Pearse (Mar-

tin, 1973)—founder of the Irish Revolutionary movement—was thrilled to observe the carnage of the First World War:

> The last sixteen months have been the most glorious in the history of Europe. Heroism has come back to the earth. It is good for the world to be warmed with the red wine of the battlefield. Such august homage was never before offered to God as this—the homage of millions of lives given gladly for love of country.

In a similar vein, the French nationalist Maurice Barrès (1918b) had this to say about his nation's soldiers who were dying on a daily basis during the First World War:

> Oh you young men whose value is so much greater than ours! They love life, but even were they dead, France will be rebuilt from their souls which are like living stones. The sublime sun of youth sinks into the sea and becomes the dawn which will hereafter rise again.

Claiming that it is "good for the world to be warmed with the red wine of the battlefield," Pearse characterizes slaughter as a form of "august homage offered to God." Barrès claims that France will be rebuilt based on the souls of dead soldiers, which are like "living stones." Each of these men—as well as many others political leaders at the time—conceived of the First World War as a form of sacrifice.

Even before the war ended, the French and British governments began creating enormous cemeteries memorializing soldiers who had died. The French lavished meticulous care upon these cemeteries—showing more endless concern for the lawns with their rows of crosses than they did for the young men that had been so promiscuously thrown into battle.

THE DUTY TO LAY DOWN ONE'S LIFE

Hitler fought in the First World War throughout its duration and witnessed the perpetual slaughter. In spite of the horrors he experienced and observed, he idealized warfare—viewing it through the prism of sacrifice. In *Mein Kampf*, Hitler stated that in the First World War the most precious blood had "sacrificed itself joyfully," in the faith that it was "preserving the independence and freedom of the fatherland." He observed that more than once, thousands and thousands of young Germans had stepped forward with "self-sacrificing resolve to sacrifice their young lives freely and joyfully on the altar of the beloved fatherland."

Germany did not exactly "lose" the First World War. Like other nations, she seemed willing to continue to send young men into the cauldron. However, after the United States entered the war, some German leaders recognized the futility of continuing to fight. The Allies had many more bodies than the Germans—that they could continue to throw into battle. Germany surrendered and signed an armistice agreement with the Allies on November 11, 1918.

Hitler was traumatized by Germany's defeat. He could not bear to acknowledge that the sacrifices had been in vain—that Germany had lost the war in spite of 2 million Germans killed and 4 million more maimed or wounded. Hitler experienced the ending of the war as a betrayal of the fighting men by the government. Politicians who negotiated the surrender in 1918 were called "November criminals."

Hitler held Jews responsible for this "stab in the back," which he never forgot nor forgave. He initiated the Second World War, it would appear, as a continuation of the First World War—in order to reverse the previous outcome. Or perhaps it is more accurate to say that Hitler generated the second war in order to perpetuate—and *to expand upon*—the sacrificial slaughter of the first war.

On September 1, 1939, Hitler declared war. How may we understand Hitler's motives and intentions? The most productive method, I have found, is simply to pay close attention to Hitler's words. The

following is an excerpt of what Hitler said as he spoke before the
Reichstag as German planes and troops crossed the Polish borders
in a devastating Blitzkrieg (Snyder, 1961):

> As a National Socialist and a German soldier, I enter
> upon this fight with a stout heart! My whole life has
> been but one continuous struggle for my people, and
> that whole struggle has been inspired by one single
> conviction: Faith in my people! I ask of every German
> what I myself am prepared to do at any moment: to
> be ready to lay down his life for his people and for
> his country. If anyone thinks that he can evade this
> national duty directly or indirectly, he will perish.

Hitler speaks in this passage not of conquest, but rather of a
"struggle" based on "faith in his people." He asks every German to
do what he is prepared to do (and eventually did): to "lay down his
life for his people and country." He goes on to say that anyone who
thinks that they can "evade this national duty" (to lay down one's
life for Germany)—would "perish."

Hitler appears to be saying that in the war that was to follow,
everyone would be required to demonstrate devotion to Germany
through a willingness to fight and die for her. On the other hand,
those seeking to evade the duty to fight and die for Germany—they
too would perish. The ideology of totalitarianism required that
everyone participate. No one was exempt from the sacrificial obligation: "Either die for Germany, or Germany will kill you."

Hitler imagined that some people did not wish to devote themselves to Germany and National Socialism. The existence of such
people acted to shatter Hitler's fantasy of a united *Gemeinschaft*.
The idea that some people did not wish to embrace the national
community enraged Hitler. He could not tolerate the idea that some
people might have no desire—might be unwilling—to sacrifice their
lives for Germany.

The Second World War was an extension of the First World War. Once again, Germans would be asked to lay down their lives for their nation. In the Second World War, however—unlike the First—the German leadership would not tolerate shirkers or war deserters. No one would be permitted to escape the sacrificial obligation. Jews too would be compelled to submit: to die when Hitler and Germany asked them to do so.

SOLDIERS AS SACRIFICIAL VICTIMS

People continually write and reflect upon the Holocaust. We are well aware of the fact that 6 million Jews perished. Much less has been written about—and we rarely reflect upon the fact—that well over 9 million Germans perished as a result of actions undertaken by the Nazi leadership (Sorge, 1986).

As the attack against Russia began, German General Gerd von Rundstedt admonished the soldier of the Second World War to emulate the examples of his brothers in the First World War and to "die in the same way": to be as strong, unswerving and obedient; to go "happily and as a matter of course to his death" (Baird, 1974). As war on the Eastern Front progressed, Goebbels was satisfied to note that German soldiers went into battle "with devotion, like congregations going into service." With rare exceptions, German soldiers did not rebel against their duty to fight and die. They went into battle "like sheep going to the slaughter."

The following passages—excerpted from letters depicting unimaginable horror and suffering (Fritz, 1997)—sound familiar:

> We were crowded together like sardines in the cattle car. There were moans, groans, and whimpers in that car; the smell of pus, urine, and it was cold. We lay on straw. The train waited for hours.

Food was our most difficult problem. Our eyes gleamed, like the eyes of famished wolves. Our stomachs were empty and the horizon was devoid of any hope.

We stood in interminable lines, to receive a cup of hot water infused with a minute portion of tea. We had too much food in order to die, but too little in order to live.

The inability to bathe led to incredibly filthy conditions, which inevitably resulted in a plague of lice. We felt like livestock rather than human beings.

There is only anxiety, fear, and terror, a life without return along with terror without an end. The heart is overwhelmed at the unbearable thought that the smell of dead bodies is the beginning and end and ultimate sense and purpose of our being.

Of course, these passages sound like they were written by Jews—describing their experience of the death camps. Actually, they are letters written home by German soldiers fighting in Russia—freezing, starving, wounded and dying in places like Stalingrad. Having vowed to be "absolutely obedient" to Adolf Hitler and to be prepared to "offer his life at any time," the German soldier did not struggle again his obligation to die—to sacrifice his life.

THE RIGHT TO DESTROY MILLIONS OF MEN

According to the logic of warfare, a nation and its leaders have the right to send young men into battle, where they may be killed or wounded. Hitler was well aware of this fact. It led him to reflect upon the following paradox: If the nation-state is allowed to undertake a project that causes its best citizens to perish, why can it not also undertake a project that causes its worst citizens to die?

The murder of Jews began on the Eastern Front in the Soviet Union before the establishment of death camps and gas chambers. The *Einsatzgruppen* (mobile killing units) followed the German army into Russia and murdered 1.5 million Jews in late 1941 and early 1942 east of the Soviet border. Hitler professed to be undisturbed by the extermination of men, women and children, declaring: "If I don't mind sending the pick of the German people into the hell of war without regret for the shedding of valuable Germany blood, then I have naturally the right to destroy millions of men of inferior races who increase like vermin" (Meltzer, 1976).

Here we approach the crux of the matter and meaning of the Holocaust. Genocide, it would appear, grew out of Hitler's meditations on the nature of warfare. He reflected: "If society gives me the right to shed the blood of Germany's most valuable citizens, why would I not also have the right to destroy its worst citizens?" "If in my role as commander-in-chief I have no compunctions about sacrificing the lives of my soldiers, why should I feel guilty about killing Jews—enemies of the German people?"

In his study of the First World War, Denis Winter (1979) writes about the experience of German soldiers as they were transported to battle in box cars:

> After the stint at base, the railway took the men toward the front line. To a generation with visual memories of the railway lines running into Hitler's death camps, tense faces peering from cattle trucks, there is something disconcerting about the imagery of this journey from base camp. The soldiers went in waggons of the same type, forty of them in each waggon, kit hanging from hoods in the roof. Death was a high probability for both generations of travelers in these cattle trucks.

The cattle trucks that took Jews to death camps were the *same cattle trucks that transported German soldiers to the Western Front during the First World War.* We have not wished to draw attention to this "disconcerting" similarity between Holocaust victims and German soldiers—each transported *en masse* to a site of slaughter.

DIE FOR GERMANY—OR BE KILLED

A sign at the entrance to Auschwitz read, "I bid you welcome. This is not a holiday resort but a labor camp. Just as our soldiers risk their lives at the front to gain victory for the Third Reich, you will have to work for the welfare of a new Europe." Hitler imagined that Jews had been "shirkers" during the First World War—had acted to avoid their obligation to fight and die for Germany. This time, Jews would not be exempt. Just as German soldiers were suffering and dying at the front, so Jews would be required to suffer and die. If German soldiers were forced to submit to the nation-state and its leaders—to undergo a horrible, painful ordeal—Jews would be forced to undergo an even more horrible, painful ordeal.

Primo Levi notes (1986) that in many of its painful and absurd aspects the concentration world was "only a version, an adaptation of German military procedure," the army of prisoners an "inglorious copy of the army proper or, more accurately, its caricature." Similarly, Leon Poliakov (1979): "Dressed in rags, the slaves had to march at parade step and with a martial air when going off to work; while other slaves played military marches. Crippled by disease, their feet running with sores, the prisoners were forced to make their beds with geometric precision." The Jew in the death camps represented a perverse version of the German soldier. It's as if prisoners were performing a *satire* on military discipline and basic training.

Although soldiers are portrayed as aggressive warriors, the actual condition of the German soldier during the First World War was one of abject submission. Jews in the death camps, I hypothesize, symbolized the German soldier in the First World War. The death camps enact the condition of a human being whose body has been taken over by the nation: compelled to be obedient unto death.

The Nazis glorified duty: willingness to surrender to Hitler and Germany. Absolute submission was conceived as honor, loyalty and faithfulness; the death of the soldier in battle as noble self-sacrifice. Newspapers reported the death of the soldier by declaring that he had died "for Fuehrer and Reich."

The Holocaust depicts suffering and death at the hands of the nation-state without sugar-coating: stripped of honor and glory. The death camps portray submission to the nation-state as abjection and degradation, enacting the horrific fate of a body that has been put at the disposal of the nation: given over to—taken over by—the state.

As Hitler asked his soldiers to sacrifice their lives for Germany, so did he require the death of Jews. The Holocaust affirmed the totalitarian principle that the state is all encompassing. During the early years of Hitler's reign, Jews had been split off—separated from the German body politic; deemed unfit to participate. The Final Solution brought Jews back into the fold. They would be included in the sacrificial ritual that Hitler brought forth.

We return to the words or prophecy uttered by Hitler in his declaration of war on September 1, 1939. Hitler began by asking every German to do what he said he was prepared to do: To lay down his life for his people. Then he went on to say: "If anyone thinks that he can evade this national duty directly or indirectly, he will perish." True to these words, Hitler carried out this policy. German soldiers who attempted to desert or civilians who tried to surrender (for example, by waving a white flag out of an apartment window when Soviet troops entered Berlin in 1945) often were shot by the SS.

Stephen Fritz (1997), in his study of war on the Eastern Front, observes that German soldiers suspected of desertion were often executed and left dangling from trees or poles with placards around their necks that read "cowardice in the face of the enemy." Sixteen-year-old Hans-Rudolf Vilter never forgot the picture of chaos in Berlin in 1945, especially the deserters and apprehended soldiers that one saw hanging on lampposts and trees with the sign, "I hang here because I am too cowardly to defend my fatherland."

To the end, Hitler refused to allow his people to surrender—to acknowledge that the war had been lost. He continued to require that his people "lay down their lives," fulfilling his prophecy that one would either die in the process of fighting for Germany, or perish. One soldier, according to Fritz, recalled with bitterness that in the fall of 1944, armed German officers gave his unit no choice but to attack enemy lines. The other option was clear: be shot by your own leaders.

Units established special formations whose instructions were to "make immediate use of their weapons in order to enforce obedience and discipline." The situation in which many German soldiers found themselves, said Helmut Altner, himself a soldier, was devilishly simple: "There were only two possibilities: Death by a bullet from the enemy, or by the 'thugs' of the SS." Thus did Hitler fulfill his dream of war and enforce the sacrificial obligation: Either die for Germany, or be killed.

PART TWO

WAR

CHAPTER III

As the Soldier Dies, So the Nation Comes Alive

INTRODUCTION

Many political events of the Twentieth Century have been characterized by massive killing, dying and destruction: for example, the First World War, Russian revolution and Soviet genocides, rise of the Nazis and genocide of the Jews, and World War II. These events—preserved in our collective consciousness by a relentless stream of books and television documentaries—lie at the core of the "history" of the Twentieth Century. We know that these events happened, but do we really know why? Do we understand the causes and meanings of these monumental episodes of destruction?

Historians conceive their fundamental task to be the description or documentation of what has occurred. Although events depicted may appear from a human perspective to be strange, irrational and bizarre, rarely are they described as strange, irrational and bizarre. Rather, historians believe that their fundamental responsibility simply is to provide facts or details about what occurred.

Wars, for example, are discussed in terms of the political machinations and economic situations that lead to the onset of battle; the nature of the fighting that occurs and strategies that govern battles; the results and consequences of warfare. The underlying assumption governing the writing of history is that there must have been good reasons for what happened. Given the bias of Western culture toward rationality, people find it difficult to imagine that historical events may have been generated by obscure, irrational forces.

Once events are written up in "history books," they become part of our world-taken-for-granted. The process of creating a historical record—of "documenting" what occurred—normalizes and confers dignity upon events, however strange and bizarre they may have been. Given the weight of monographs and texts, people begin to assume that there must have been good reasons for what occurred.

The assumption that we actually understand societal mass destruction in my view is unfounded. We begin to reconceptualize the historical process by acknowledging that we *do not actually know the causes of what occurred*. The destruction of life and property on such a vast scale during the Twentieth Century cannot be explained in conventional economic and political terms. To understand these events, we must consider the possibility that the historical process is governed by profoundly irrational forces.

OBFUSCATION IN THE DEPICTION OF WARFARE

I wish to interrogate the ideology that supports the willingness of a soldier to "die for his country," that is, a soldier's willingness to enter battle knowing there is a possibility or probability that he will be killed or wounded. The Roman poet Horace proposed that it is "sweet and fitting to die for one's country." Nationalists put forth propositions such as "the individual must die so that the nation might live." What is the meaning of this ideology that views dying for one's country as necessary and beautiful?

Inherent within the institution of warfare is a tendency toward obfuscation: the will to avoid looking closely at what happens in battle. Accounts of warfare in history books and the media turn away from a full encounter with the consequences of battle: the dead or mutilated bodies of soldiers. Further, there is a blandness or conventionality about how people think about and describe warfare. Astonishing, strange and horrific things often occur. Yet accounts of battle rarely convey a sense of astonishment, strangeness or horror.

Up until 1989, the focus of my research was Hitler, Nazism, genocide and the Holocaust. Having read many of the books on this topic at the New York University library, I strolled over to stacks on the opposite side of the aisle and began leafing through books on the First World War. I was shocked to discover the massive carnage and surprised by the battle strategy that dominated the war—how men day after day, month after month, year after year got out of trenches and were slaughtered—cut down by machine-gun fire and artillery shells. I was bewildered by the inexplicable destructiveness and by the fact that people allowed the war to keep going.

Equally surprising was the casualness or nonchalant tone with which historians reported these events. Were they not horrified and amazed by the endless slaughter? It seemed that they made little effort to step back and question what was going on—to interrogate the meaning of the slaughter. The First World War was a horrendous, chaotic, brutal, and often surrealistically absurd war. One gets the feeling that something unnatural and abnormal was occurring. Yet the war is portrayed as if a more-or-less natural or normal event. Historians describe the quantity and persistence of the killing and dying and the suicidal nature of the battle strategies, but rarely step back and ask: What was going on? What was the death and maiming all about?

More generally, people avoid looking closely at the horror of warfare. We shield ourselves from reality—the anguish of knowing what occurs in battle—by telling ourselves that warfare is a firmly established form of social behavior that has existed since the beginning of civilization (and well before the beginning of civilization). We reassure ourselves that because warfare has occurred so frequently, therefore it is "normal."

We need not be disturbed by the massive death and maiming that occurred in the First World War, or in any other war for that matter. Why become surprised or upset? Societies have been waging war for thousands of years. Why act as if what occurred was unusual or extraordinary?

Denial of the reality of what happens in battle is reflected in the way warfare has been portrayed in documentaries and movies throughout the years. In the past 30 years, we have witnessed a significant change in this regard—as movies and documentaries have become much more realistic in their depictions of warfare. However, reflecting on the World War II documentaries that I witnessed as a youth (for example, *Victory at Sea*), I am amazed when I recall how infrequently I saw soldiers killed or being maimed.

I'm thinking specifically of films of the naval battles in the Pacific between the United States and Japan. Bombs were dropped on aircraft carriers, artillery shells fired, and airplanes plunged into the ocean. But how rarely did we witness the human cost. On the basis of these documentaries, it seemed that war was a glorious Fourth of July celebration: The rockets' red glare, bombs bursting in air.

World War II documentaries depicted war as an exciting event that one might very much like to be part of: soldiers marching off to a foreign land with crowds cheering; bands playing and women providing support and encouragement; heroic landings on beaches; massive, magnificent ships; airplanes soaring and dropping bombs. Occasionally, one notices someone falling to the ground.

However, such a detail paled in comparison to the overall splendor conveyed. Based on the newsreels, documentaries and movies about World War II produced in the Forties, Fifties and Sixties, one comes away with the impression that war is something wonderful: an exciting display of energy; an event that makes one proud to be part of such a powerful, efficient and well-organized nation.

I suggest that conventional representations of war function as distancing mechanisms that allow us to avoid a close encounter with what happens to the bodies of soldiers. These distancing mechanisms—denial of the actuality of death and mutilation—are part and parcel of the institution of warfare. People are attached to the *idea* of war, but *don't want to know what happens to the human body as a result of warfare.*

As I describe the details of the First World War, please try to recover a sense of innocence. If what I describe does not seem to make sense, do not assume that it does make sense. Do not assume that historians—or anyone else—knew or knows what was going on. If what I describe sounds bizarre, strange and abnormal, do not assume that what occurred was not bizarre, strange and abnormal— simply because it is written up in history books.

THE MAGNITUDE OF DESTRUCTION AND FUTILITY OF THE FIRST WORLD WAR

To convey a sense of the magnitude of the destructiveness of World War I, I provide the following statistics from a U. S. War Department table entitled "Casualties of All Belligerents in World War I." Data is provided for the Allied nations, which included Russia, France, the British Commonwealth, Italy and the United States; and for the Central Powers, namely Germany, Austria-Hungary, Turkey and Bulgaria. According to the U. S. War Department, there were a total of 65,038,315 forces—people that is—mobilized to fight in this war.

Of the forces mobilized (civilians excluded), 8,538,315 were killed or died; 21,219,452 were wounded; and 7,750,919 were taken prisoner or reported missing. Total casualties (the number of human beings killed, wounded, taken prisoner or reported missing) in other words were 37,508,686, or 57.7% of all forces mobilized. For some nations, the percentage of casualties reached astounding proportions. For Austria-Hungary, for example, of 7,800,000 forces mobilized, 7,020,000 or 90% were casualties; for Russia, 76.3% of 12 million forces were casualties; for France, 73.3% of 8,410,000 forces were casualties.

The magnitude of destruction that occurred in the First World War is matched by the extraordinary way in which many battles were fought. On the Western Front, much of the fighting was done out of trenches, with one enemy line facing the other. "Attack" occurred when long rows of soldiers got out of a trench and moved into No Man's Land—running or walking as they advanced toward the enemy line. The enemy was equipped with machine-guns. With unimpeded vision, machine-gunners could mow down approaching troops with small risk to themselves.

There was a substantial probability that an attacking soldier would be hit by an artillery shell or riddled with bullets from machine-guns. Here is the way historian Modris Eksteins (1989) describes the typical pattern of battles that occurred on the Western Front in France during the First World War:

> The victimized crowd of attackers in no man's land has become one of the supreme images of this war. Attackers moved forward usually without seeking cover and were mowed down in rows, with the mechanical efficiency of a scythe, like so many blades of grass. "We were very surprised to see them walking," wrote a German machine-gunner of his experience of a British attack at the Somme. "The officers went in front. I noticed one of them walking calmly, carrying a walking stick. When we started firing we just had to load and reload. They went down in the hundreds. You didn't have to aim, we just fired into them." A Frenchman described the effects of his machine-gunners more laconically: "The Germans fell like cardboard soldiers."

The following is an account of the British attack at Loos in September 1915 that appeared in the German 15th Reserve Regiment's diary:

> Ten ranks of extended line could clearly be
> distinguished, each one estimated at more than a
> thousand men, and offering such a target as had never
> been seen before, or even thought possible. Never had
> the machine-gunners such straight-forward work to
> do nor done it so effectively.

The enormous number of troops killed and vast proportion of casualties was a logical consequence of this method of fighting.

Eksteins describes the results of some of the early (1914) battles: German and French casualties had been staggering. The Germans lost a million men in the first five months. France, in the "battle of the frontiers" of August, lost over 300,000 men in two weeks. Some regiments lost three-quarters of their men in the first month. Total French losses by the end of December 1914 were comparable with the German, roughly 300,000 killed and 600,000 wounded or missing. At Mons, Le Cateau, and then especially at Ypres most of the original British Expeditionary Force of 160,000 had been wiped out. As an example of the scale of casualties, the 11th Brigade of the British Expeditionary Force had, by December 20, only 18% of its original officers left and 28% of its men.

Eksteins concludes that during the first two years of war, the belligerents on the Western Front "hammered at each other in battles that cost millions of men their lives but moved the front line at most a mile or so in either direction." The war that began in August 1914 finally ended in November 1918. If one substitutes "four years" for "two years" in the sentence above, Eksteins' conclusion is one with which most historians would concur. In short, after hundreds of battles in which millions of soldiers were killed or maimed, little had changed from a military or political standpoint, apart from the fact that now millions of young men were dead or maimed.

WHAT WAS GOING ON?

As I've noted, historians until recently have been complacent in their analysis of the First World War. They assume simply that soldiers will "do their duty." Yet what a radical form of behavior this was—getting out of a trench and running into machine-gun fire. The behavior of soldiers in the First World War contradicts our assumptions about an "instinct for survival." Eksteins interrogates the meaning of the First World War by raising questions about the behavior of soldiers:

> What kept them in the trenches? What sustained them on the edge of No Man's Land, that strip of territory which death ruled with an iron fist? What made them go over the top, in long rows? What sustained them in constant confrontation with death?

Eksteins notes that we are talking not of professional armies but of mass armies, of volunteers and conscripts in numbers that the world had never seen before.

The incidence of insubordination and sedition was minuscule in relation to the number of men under arms and in view of the conditions they had to brave. The question of what kept men going in this hell of the Western Front, Eksteins says, is "central to an understanding of the war and its significance." He summarizes the fundamental question as follows:

> What deserves emphasis in the context of the war is that, despite the growing dissatisfaction, the war continued, and it continued for one reason: the soldier was willing to keep fighting. Just why he kept going has to be explained, and that matter has often been ignored.

Political scientist Jean Elshtain (1987) is another scholar who draws our attention to the question of what was going on during World War I. She observes that the First World War was the "nadir of nineteenth-century nationalism." Mounds of bodies were sacrificed in a "prolonged, dreadful orgy of destruction." "Trench warfare" it was called and it meant "mass, anonymous death." In the first day of the Battle of the Somme, July 1, 1916, Elshtain notes, 60,000 men were killed or wounded of the 110,000 on the British side who got out of the trenches and began to walk forward along a 13-mile front.

Elshtain places questions about the First World War within the framework of broader questions about nationalism, war and mass-death. She observes that we "still have trouble accounting for modern state worship;" the "mounds of combatants and noncombatants alike sacrificed to the conflicts of nation-states." Ronald Aronson (1983) also raises this larger question of the persistence and meaning of mass-death in warfare:

> In contemplating history as the slaughter-bench at which the happiness of peoples, the wisdom of States, and the virtue of the individual have been sacrificed, a question necessarily arises: To what principle, to what purpose, have these monstrous sacrifices been made?

Elshtain and Aronson point us in the direction of explanatory concepts. Elshtain speaks of "modern state worship" and of combatants being "sacrificed to the conflicts of nation-states," while Aronson suggests viewing history as a slaughter-bench requiring "monstrous sacrifices."

REIFICATION OF THE NATION-STATE

The idea that "the individual must die so that the nation might live" has been put forth frequently in the course of the history of

Western nationalism. This phrase reifies the nation-state, treating nations not as social constructions but as if objects that substantially exist. The phrase suggests that countries exist as entities in their own right, separate and distinct from the individuals or human beings that reside within them. If nations are not equivalent to the people who are contained within them, however, what is it that "lives" when a nation lives?

So pervasive is the ideology of nationalism that when speaking of "France" or "Germany" or "America," we must remind ourselves that these words refer to ideas or concepts created by human beings rather than to concrete objects or entities that substantially exist. A statement like "The individual must die so that the nation might live" suggests that nations have a life of their own; as if countries are living creatures, the preservation of which is more significant or valuable than the preservation of the lives of actual human beings.

In war, human bodies are sacrificed in the name of perpetuating a magical entity, the body politic. Sacrificial acts function to affirm the reality or existence of this sacred object, the nation. Entering into battle may be characterized as a devotional act, with death in war constituting the supreme act of devotion.

Maurice Barrès (1918a, 1918b) was a prominent French nationalist who published several books during the course of the First World War containing letters written by French soldiers—to their parents, relatives and friends—before entering battle. Many of the soldiers whose letters were preserved and cited by Barrès subsequently were killed. The following is a typical excerpt (1918b) written by French soldier George Morillot—who died on December 11, 1914—to his parents:

> If this letter comes into your hands it will be because I am no more and because I shall have died the most glorious of deaths. Do not bewail me too much; my end is the most to be desired. Speak of me from time to time

as of one of those men who have given their blood that France may live and who has died gladly.

Since my earliest childhood I have always dreamed of dying for my country. Let me sleep where the accident of battle shall have placed me, by the side of those who, like myself, shall have died for France; I shall sleep well there. My dear Father and Mother, happy are those who die for their native land. What matters the life of individuals if France is saved?

The phrase "What matters the life of individuals if France is saved" contains the essence of the ideology that generated the First World War and allowed it to continue. People imagined that they were fighting in order to rescue the life of their own nation. The French soldier above writes about the French nation as if it were a concrete, tangible entity whose "life" is more valuable than his own.

He proclaims that he wishes to be remembered as one of those men who has "given their blood that France might live." This image evokes a blood transfusion—where the life-sustaining substance of an individual body passes into a collective body, acting to keep it alive. What is the nature of this structure of thought or fantasy that gives rise to the belief that the death of the soldier—his offering of blood—functions to keep one's nation alive?

WILLINGNESS TO DIE AS DECLARATION OF DEVOTION

As soldiers may be willing to give over their bodies to their countries, so do national leaders and non-combatants applaud or extol the virtue of these young men who demonstrate a willingness to sacrifice their lives for the sake of their nations. Here is what Maurice Barrès (1918a) had to say about French soldiers dying on a daily basis during the First World War:

Nothing more beautiful yet more difficult to understand than these boys, today cold in their graves, who gave themselves for France. With all the strength of their young lives they urged preparedness; they foresaw that this would be their own downfall, yet joyously they rushed to meet it.

And here are the words of P. H. Pearse (Martin, 1973), founder of the Irish revolutionary movement, upon observing the daily carnage in France:

The last sixteenth months have been the most glorious in the history of Europe. Heroism has come back to the earth. It is good for the world that such things should be done. The old heart of the earth needed to be warmed with the red wine of the battlefield. Such august homage was never before offered to God as this, the homage of millions of lives given gladly for love of country.

How extraordinary to hear prominent political figures in the Twentieth Century declaring that soldiers in war "joyously" rushed to meet their downfall and that the heart of the earth needed to be "warmed with the red wine of the battlefield." Yet images like these convey the thought processes that sustained four years of warfare, or slaughter. Perhaps Pearse's words unlock the meaning of the First World War. Perhaps this war represented a massive sacrificial ritual—millions of lives "given gladly for love of country."

Willingness to enter battle manifests devotion to one's nation: a "pledge of allegiance" in its most radical form. A reporter during the First World War recalled an encounter with a wounded Canadian soldier:

As I looked into his face and saw the look of personal victory over physical pain, I gripped him by the hand

and said: "My good man, when you go back home to
Canada, back to your home, you need not tell them that
you love your country, that you love your home—just
show them your scars."

Wounds function as a testimonial, allowing one to prove to non-combatants that one's devotion is sincere. "Scars" constitute the form in which the soldier declares that he loves his country.

AS THE SOLDIER DIES, SO THE NATION COMES ALIVE

Barrès (1918b) claimed that the French make war as a "religious duty." He says that French soldiers "die for France," waging war in the "spirit of martyrs." He cites Roland in the medieval *Song of Roland* murmuring with dying breath: "O Land of France, most sweet are thou, my country" and claims that it was with "similar expressions and the same love" that French soldiers were dying in the First World War.

Barrès reproduces a letter written by Jean Cherlomey to his wife before entering battle: "Au revoir. Promise to bear no grudge against France if she requires all of me." He says that the dying words of Captain de La Villemarque were "Au revoir, it is for the sake of France" and that Corporal Voituret declared before he died, "Vive la France, I am well content; I am dying for her sake."

Though these declarations of devotion to one's nation sound archaic, they articulate the psychological dynamic that lies at the heart of the ideology of nationalism and war. Why does Corporal Voituret proclaim "Long live France" before he dies in battle? In what sense does the death of a soldier endow one's nation with more abundant life? War may be viewed as a sacrificial ritual that valorizes the nation-state. It is as if death in battle functions to transfer energy within a human body—the life-force contained within the body of a soldier—into a body politic, endowing the nation with renewed vigor. As the soldier dies, so the nation comes alive.

In her study of the image of the Western soldier, Elshtain found that the warrior or combatant presents himself in his most proto-typical guise "not as a bloodthirsty militant." Rather, by his own account of wartime experience, he constructs himself as one who places the highest value "not on killing but on dying—dying for others." Elshtain cites the writings of J. Glenn Gray (1998) who examined the impulse to self-sacrifice characteristic of warriors who from compassion would "rather die than kill." Gray calls the freedom of wartime a communal freedom "as the 'I' passes into a 'we'," and human longing for community with others "finds a field for realization." Communal ecstasy, Elshtain says, explains the will-ingness to sacrifice and "gives dying for others a mystical quality."

We've observed that the central battle strategy of the First World War consisted of unrelenting attacks upon the enemy front that almost always were futile and resulted in an astonishingly high rate of casualties. The *Australian Official History*—discussing one such battle that resulted in 23,000 casualties—angrily condemned the battle strategy of "throwing several parts of an army corps, brigade after brigade, twenty times in succession against one of the stron-gest points in the enemy's defense." The problem, however, Eksteins observes, was that the determination and grit of a unit came to be measured by the number of casualties: "Officers whose companies incurred light casualties were suspect, so they pressed their attacks with appropriate vigor."

Large numbers of battle-casualties testified to the sincerity of the effort: demonstrated the depth of one's devotion to the sacred ideal, one's nation. When an officer led an attack that produced few casualties, it was as if he was insufficiently sincere—lacked faith in the cause. According to this perverse logic, an officer's performance was evaluated in terms of the number of casualties that occurred during battle. If only a few casualties were incurred, the officer might be judged to have not tried hard enough; whereas a large number of casualties testified to the magnitude of his devotion.

CHAPTER IV

Virility and Slaughter

INTRODUCTION

Historians estimate that during the First World War (1914-1918), 9 million soldiers were killed, 21 million wounded, and nearly 8 million taken prisoner or reported missing. Thus, of 65 million troops mobilized, nearly 38 million, or 58 percent were casualties. What was the purpose and meaning of this war? Why were millions of young men slaughtered?

Perhaps we can begin to comprehend this case of civilizational self-destruction by examining the central strategy that guided the course of battles: that of the "offensive at all costs." This "strategy," it would appear, actually represented an ideology. The belief that it was worthwhile for soldiers to attack whenever possible (the offensive at all costs) derived from the idea that morale and discipline were the crucial factors determining success on the battlefield. A nation could achieve victory, according to this philosophy, only if troops had the courage and will to move forward relentlessly—to continue to attack even in the face of heavy casualties.

47

THE FIRST WORLD WAR AS PERPETUAL SLAUGHTER

When I began my research on the First World War and encountered the perpetual, futile slaughter that characterized this war, I assumed that historians were capable of accounting for what had occurred; that there must have been a logical explanation. My assumption was unfounded. Historians describe the events—provide a report of what occurred—but are unable to comprehend the meaning of the war. Why did the killing persist for four years despite the fact that nothing was accomplished?

Jay Winter—one of the best and most prominent historians of the First World War—concludes his six-part video series (*The Great War and the Shaping of the 20th Century*, 1996) in a tone of baffled bewilderment, summing up his reflections as follows: "The war solved no problems. Its effects, both immediate and indirect, were either negative or disastrous. Morally subversive, economically destructive, socially degrading, confused in its course, futile in its result, it is the outstanding example in European history of meaningless conflict."

Studying the battles of the First World War, one learns of the prodigious number of human beings that were killed in each of them. The mind boggles. What was going on? What kept the war going? Why did leaders persist in asking young men to get out of trenches and run into artillery shells and machine-gun fire? Why didn't the Generals modify their battle strategy after it had become evident that what they were doing did not work? Why did soldiers rarely rebel? Why did they continue to fight on even as death stared them in the face?

The First World War began with Germany moving through Belgium to attack France, expecting a quick victory that did not occur. The French counterattack also failed. Britain joined the war to honor its treaty obligation with Belgium. Soon there was stalemate. The combatants then built 500 miles of zigzagging trenches in France. Soldiers settled in on opposing lines, sometimes separated by distances of only 100-300 yards. Which side would give in first?

The high casualty rate during this war reflected the nature of the battle strategy. "Attack" occurred when massive numbers of troops along the front line—supported by artillery fire from thousands of guns—got out of their trenches and ran into No Man's Land toward the enemy trench. Generals hoped that their troops would be able to cut the barbed wire that protected enemy troops, assault them in their trenches, and break through the opposing line.

Attacks were nearly always unsuccessful. Here is Eksteins' (1989) description of the fundamental pattern:

> The victimized crowd of attackers in No Man's Land has become one of the supreme images of this war. Attackers moved forward usually without seeking cover and were mowed down in rows, with the mechanical efficiency of a scythe, like so many blades of grass. "We were very surprised to see them walking," wrote a German machine-gunner of his experience of a British attack at the Somme. "The officers went in front. I noticed one of them walking calmly, carrying a walking stick. When we started firing, we just had to load and reload. They went down in the hundreds. You didn't have to aim, we just fired into them."

Eksteins describes the results of the first year of fighting on the Western Front, 1914:

> German and French casualties had been staggering. The Germans lost a million men in the first five months. France, in the "battle of the frontiers" of August, lost over 300,000 men in two weeks. Total French losses by the end of December were comparable with the German, roughly 300,000 killed and 600,000 wounded or missing.

What did all of this killing and dying accomplish? Eksteins writes: "For over two years the belligerents on the Western Front hammered at each other in battles that cost millions of men their lives but moved the front line at most a mile or so in either direction."

DOCTRINE OF THE "OFFENSIVE AT ALL COSTS"

How may one account for the monumental and futile destructiveness that characterized the First World War? How may one explain the fact that national governments and their military leaders persisted in employing a battle strategy that continually failed while costing millions of men their lives? Perhaps one may begin to grasp what occurred by examining the battle doctrine that guided the thinking of many British officers, as well as military leaders of other European nations.

This doctrine of the "offensive at all costs" grew out of the Russo-Japanese war of 1904-1905 (see Miller et al., 1991; Terraine, 1982; Travers, 1987). The Japanese sent wave after wave of troops against Russian lines in the face of machine-guns. Casualties were enormous, but eventually Russian troops were overwhelmed by the persistent Japanese attacks. European officers who studied the war were impressed by the "morale and discipline" of the Japanese soldiers: their capacity or willingness to push or move forward relentlessly in spite of heavy casualties.

Thus evolved a paradigm that fixed or focused on the "psychological battlefield" as the key element of warfare. The issue, according to this doctrine, was whether troops had the courage and will to cross the fire-swept zone, suffer heavy casualties in the attack and still keep going—moving forward (Travers, 1987). The doctrine of the offensive was put forth as an antidote to modern fire power. Precisely because modern fire power made the offensive so difficult, therefore the offense had to be heavily overemphasized (Travers, 1987). This strategy was likely to be very costly in manpower in the face of modern weapons such as machine-guns. The doctrine of the offensive must take account of this—and still remain offensive.

Remarkably, it sometimes was suggested that offensive tactics must actually *aim* at heavy losses, since this was the most reliable and sure way of getting through enemy defenses (Travers, 1987). In the First World War film, *Paths of Glory* (1957, directed by Stanley Kubrick), the French General justifies the ruthless tactic of requiring his soldiers to attack in the face of machine-guns by explaining that soldiers on the front line of the assault "absorb bullets and shrapnel and by doing so allow other men to get through."

Given a battle strategy guided by the philosophy of the offensive at all costs, British officers who did not encourage the offensive spirit often were removed. In 1918, General Sir Hubert Grough complained to his aide that his troops had "no blood lust" and his officers no "spirit of the offensive." He told his aide: "I want to shoot two officers." The aide replied, "Beg your pardon, Sir, there are no officers under sentence." Grough looked at him as if to say, "You fool," and explained, "Yes, I know that, but I want to shoot two officers as an example to others." Two officers were shot (Travers, 1987).

Officers' fears that they could be executed or removed gave General Headquarters considerable leverage. Faced with obviously hopeless attacks, commanding officers were reluctant to complain and felt compelled to attack regardless of circumstances (Travers, 1987). Attacks that failed with considerable casualties were given a sympathetic hearing, whereas attacks that failed with light casualties inevitably were condemned. If a Brigadier lost a position, he might be removed—not for losing the position—but for not losing enough men in trying to hold it. General Douglas Haig castigated Division 49 for not holding Ancre in September 1916 complaining, "Total losses of this division are under a thousand!" (Travers, 1987).

THE BATTLE OF THE SOMME

In 1916, the British felt that they had found a commander-in-chief with the courage and resolve to sustain the heavy losses that would be necessary to break through the German line. General Douglas Haig (De Groot, 1988) believed that—given an adequate supply of arms and men—victory could be achieved quickly, though not without great loss of life. The specter of massive losses did not deter him. Haig said that what was needed for victory were patriots who "knew the importance of the cause for which we were fighting."

Whereas Germans, Haig said, had been impregnated from youth up with an intensely patriotic feeling so that they "willingly die for their country," British men could not do this unless well led. Haig believed that this simple fact had escaped the King who—during a visit to the front—seemed inclined to think that "our troops are by nature brave." Haig was annoyed by the fact that the King seemed to be ignorant of all the efforts commanders had to make to keep up the morale of their men and all the training necessary to enable a company to "go forward as a unit in the face of almost certain death."

British strategy was set forth in a document written by General Montgomery dated April 11, 1916, which asserted that assaulting troops must "push forward at a steady pace in successive lines, each line adding fresh impetus to the preceding line." Although two or three lines of attack *sometimes* succeed, this document asserted, four or more lines *usually* succeed (Travers, 1987).

"War," Lieutenant General Ian Hamilton declared, is the triumph of "one will over another weaker will." According to the theory of the offensive at all costs, victory essentially was a question of morale, belonging to the side that could cross the fire-swept zone and persist in the attack in spite of heavy casualties. Such a determined assault would unnerve the enemy, delivering a decisive moral and physical blow (Travers, 1987).

In July 1916, British forces amassed along a 30-mile front near the Somme River, hoping to achieve a breakthrough. Haig said that if you tried for a great, decisive victory, it would be necessary to get your men killed. An extraordinary artillery shelling preceded the attack. For several weeks, 100,000 shells a day were fired. It seemed impossible that German soldiers could survive such a massive barrage. Hiding themselves deep within their trenches or bunkers, however, most did survive. When the British attacked, German soldiers rushed to their machine-gun posts and gunned down the advancing troops.

The July 1, 1916 attack on the Somme was a disaster, the worst day in British military history, with 20,000 dead and 40,000 wounded. The results of the Battle of the Somme, however, were not unlike the course of the Battle of the Loos, which took place in September and October of 1915. Pushing through to the German line on the second day of battle, British troops crossed the road. Their numerical superiority was considerable, but several dozen German machine-guns faced them. The German regimental diary describes what happened:

> Ten columns of extended line could clearly be discerned. Each advancing column was estimated at more than a thousand men, offering such a target as had never been seen before, or thought possible. Never had the machine-gunners such straightforward work to do nor done it so effectively. They traversed to and fro along the enemy's ranks unceasingly. The men stood and fired triumphantly into the mass of men advancing across open grassland. As the entire field of fire was covered with the enemy's infantry, the effect was devastating and they could be seen falling literally in hundreds.

These were not atypical results of the British strategy of the "offensive at all costs." Was the Somme campaign called off after the first few disastrous days? On the contrary, it continued for five months, with horrible scenes like those described above occurring again and again. During the second week, the British were losing 10,000 men—an entire division per day—and for the remainder of the battle the daily average was 2500 men.

VIRILITY—THE BATTLE OF VERDUN

Another spectacle of mass-slaughter took place in 1916 at Verdun. German General von Falkenhayn—convinced that the symbolic significance of the forts at Verdun would compel the French to defend them to the last man—told Kaiser Wilhelm that whether the forts were captured or not, French forces would "bleed to death," thus permitting Germany to emerge victorious. General von Falkenhayn's statement—that he would cause the forces of France to bleed to death—is one of the most famous (or notorious) of the First World War, crystallizing an underlying assumption guiding this "war of attrition." The losing side in this war would be the one that ran out of men first. The war would end when one side or another had no more blood to give.

One French officer conceived of the Battle of Verdun as nothing less than a pure contest of French and German masculinity. The two races, he said, have put "all their youth into the furnace, to test which is the strongest and most virile." For their initial attack at Verdun, the Germans brought up 2.5 million shells, using for the purpose some 1,300 trains. By June, the artillery had grown to about 2,000 guns. It was calculated that in just over four months of battle, a million shells had been pumped into this dedicated stretch of ground, an average of 100 shells per minute.

The French action to recapture the famous Fort Douaumont employed 711 guns on a front of just over three miles. A notice in the fort today informs us that 1,000 shells were used for every square meter of the battlefield. Verdun was captured by the Germans—then recaptured by the French—so nothing changed except that there were 650,000 more dead soldiers. When added to that of the Somme, this made a death toll in 1916 of almost a million men; an average of more than 6,600 men killed every day, more than 277 every hour, nearly five men a minute.

Imagine the pathetic plight of those who were on the battlefield at Verdun, confined within a narrow space that glowed like an oven for miles because of the constant artillery bombing. During battles, most soldiers barely knew what was going on, spending most of their time hiding from the incessant shelling and bombardment of rifles and machine-gun fire rather than actually fighting.

A French Lieutenant described his situation: "Nearly all of our trench has caved in. In what remains, we have scraped our niches in the walls. We huddle up in them to get at least a bit of shelter from the explosions, but we are so tightly packed that our sore limbs can't move." He notes that before attacking his men were either "drunk, howling out patriotic airs, or weeping with emotion or despair." One had the temerity to remark within earshot of the company commander: "Baa, baa, I am the sheep on the way to the slaughterhouse."

We have noted that an officer called the battle of Verdun a test to determine which of the two races—French or German—was the most virile. What a delusion, conceiving the behavior of soldiers in the First World War as a form of virility. What virility amounted to in practice was the capacity to endure in the face of endless, perpetual slaughter. Virility was equivalent to being willing to die when one's nation asked one to do so. The soldier is often represented as the embodiment of active masculinity. The actual stance of the soldier at the battle of Verdun, however, was one of abject passivity.

Soldiers during the First World War—those of every nation—were expected to obey their officers and to do their duty without shirking; to offer no resistance when they were ordered to put their bodies onto the battlefield to face mutilation and death. The "strength" of a soldier amounted to his willingness to submit to the leadership absolutely and resign entirely to his fate. To be virile, in short, was to offer no resistance when one was put forward as a sacrificial victim.

THE SACRED IDEAL

Gwynne Dyer in his classic study *War* (1985) cites General John Winthrop Hacket: "You offer yourself to be slain: This is the essence of being a soldier. By becoming soldiers, men agree to die when we tell them to." Joanna Bourke in *Dismembering the Male* (1996) observes that the most important point to be made about the male body during the Great War is that it was "intended to be mutilated." She notes that there was "no limit to the danger to which the male body could be subjected. Gunfire cut bodies in half." In war, male bodies are turned over to the nation-state, and military leaders use these bodies as they see fit.

Why are the state and its military leaders allowed to take control of the bodies of soldiers? What justifies the mutilation and destruction of the male body? Underlying everything that occurs is the sacred ideal: one's country or nation. The destruction of the male body in the First World War occurred in the name of entities or objects given names such as France, Germany, Great Britain, Russia, Italy, etc. These objects required or justified abject submission.

In a lecture that formed an important part of their training (Kerr, 1993), Colonel Shirley told British officers that the words that he was about to speak would be among the most "serious you will ever hear in all your lives." Now that you have entered upon the service of your Country, Colonel Shirley said, you must proceed to "serve her with all your heart and with all your soul and with all your mind and with all your strength." He consoled his officers by telling them that if they have done their best and yet must fall, they might take comfort in the thought they will have suffered for a cause "greater and more noble than that for which any man has ever yet sacrificed his all."

Patriotic rhetoric resonated. One million volunteers joined the British army in the first year of the war. War Office recruiting stands were inundated with men persuaded of their duty to fight. On September 9, 1915, Basil Hart wrote to his parents asking them not to wear mourning clothes in the event of his death: "I do not wish you to regard my death as an occasion for grief, but of one for thanksgiving, for no man could desire a nobler end than to die for his country and the cause of civilization."

Eight months of battle did not alter these noble sentiments. On May 27, 1916, Hart appended the following words to his will: "Also I wish to say that while I feel it an honor to die for England, I feel it an even greater honor to die as an officer of the British Regular Army—many of the finest gentlemen whom God has sent into this world." Similar sentiments of commitment and devotion were common among soldiers of all nations. Shortly before his death, Frenchman Robert Dubarle wrote of the glorious privilege of "sacrificing oneself, voluntarily. Let us try, without complaining too much, to offer our sacrifice to our country and to place the love of fatherland above our own grief."

Willingness to join the military in the First World War—to enter battle and if necessary to die—was the way in which one demonstrated one's devotion to one's nation: the sacred ideal. To fight for one's nation—risking bodily mutilation and death—represented a pledge of allegiance in its most radical form. A reporter described his encounter with a Canadian soldier who had been wounded in battle, but survived:

> As I looked into his face and saw the look of personal victory over physical pain, I gripped him by the hand and said, "My good man, when you go back to your home, you need not tell them that you love your country—just show them your scars."

In Great Britain, according to Bourke, soldiers' mutilations were spoken of in public rhetoric as badges of courage: hallmark of their glorious service and proof of patriotism. The wounded or disabled soldier was "not less but more of a man." According to the *London Times*, next to the loss of life, the "sacrifice of a limb is the greatest sacrifice a man can make for his country."

The virtue of surrendering a body part to one's nation was expressed in a song entitled "England's Broken Dolls" that was popular during the war (Bourke, 1996):

A man and maiden met a month ago.
She said, "There's one thing I should like to know
Why aren't you in khaki or navy blue?
And fighting for your country like other men do?
The man looked up and slowly shook his head
Dear Madam, do you know what you have said.
For I gladly took my chance.
Now my right arm's out in France.

VIRILITY AND SLAUGHTER

I've provided accounts of how British soldiers were torn apart by machine-gun fire as they moved forward to attack the opposing enemy trench. In the following report, British Brigadier General Rees describes a battle in which his own brigade was massacred as they advanced on German lines:

> They advanced in line after line, dressed as if on parade and not a man shirked going through the extremely heavy barrage, or facing the machine-gun and rifle fire that finally wiped them out. I saw the lines, which advanced in such admirable order melting away under fire. Yet not a man wavered, broke the ranks, or attempted to come back. I have never seen, indeed could never have imagined such a magnificent display of gallantry, discipline and determination. The reports from the very few survivors of this marvelous advance bear out what I saw with my own eyes: that hardly a man of ours got to the German Front line.

In spite of the total failure of this attack, it is evident that General Rees regarded the destruction of his brigade in a positive light (Travers, 1987). He observes that not a man "shirked" in the face of the machine-gun and rifle fire that wiped them out. He is proud of the fact that even though his troops were "melting away under fire," they continued to advance "in admirable order." In the face of the barrage of bullets, his men did not waver, break ranks, or attempt to come back. The General gushes that he had never seen such a magnificent display of "gallantry, discipline and determination." Although his soldiers were slaughtered and "hardly a man of ours got to the German Front line," he characterizes the advance as "marvelous."

The General does not evaluate this battle from the perspective of success or failure. Rather, his observations are based on judgments revolving around the morale and spirit demonstrated by his troops. The fact that his soldiers continued to advance in spite of the fact that they were being riddled with bullets leads General Rees to conclude that the attack had been "marvelous."

The General responded positively to the slaughter of his own men because he viewed their behavior as a testimony to the depth of their devotion to their nation. By virtue of the fact that they did not shirk but continued to advance in the face of machine-gun fire, his troops demonstrated that they were absolutely committed to the ideals of Great Britain, the British Empire and its leaders. Willingness to walk into machine-gun fire represented definitive proof that his soldiers loved their country.

Soldiers during the First World War were required to adopt a posture of absolute submission to their nation and its leaders—obedience unto death. Conscientious objectors in Britain during the war were disenfranchised. Some thought that soldiers who had not seen overseas service should have the right to vote taken away from them. In the First World War, the social consensus was that bodies of soldiers belonged to the nation-state. The nation could use these bodies as it saw fit.

War requires that soldiers hand themselves over to the nation-state. In order to encourage men to allow the state to use their bodies, the soldier's role is described in positive terms with words such as honor, duty, masculinity and virility. In the First World War, however, to be honorable, masculine and virile—willing to do one's duty—was equivalent to entering a situation where there was substantial probability that one would be slaughtered.

One demonstrated one's virility by getting out of a trench and walking into artillery bombardment and machine-gun fire. Such is the paradox of war: That goodness or morality requires a posture of abject submission; that love of country requires self-destruction; that willingness to die constitutes the highest form of virtue.

CHAPTER V

Aztec Warfare, Western Warfare

AZTEC WARFARE

The Aztecs conceived of warfare as a "sacred activity" whose purpose was to capture enemy soldiers in order to sacrifice them to the gods. War was required in order to provide food and energy for the sun so that it could continue on its course. When the four original gods decided to create the sun, Burr Brundage (1985) states, they first had to "create war so that the hearts and blood needed by the sun would be available." According to Jacques Soustell (1970), the Aztecs believed that the sun was born "from sacrifice and blood."

When the hand-to-hand fighting began in a typical Mexican war, Soustell explains, the battle took on an aspect completely unlike anything known in Western civilization. The purpose was not to kill the enemy, but to capture him so that he could be offered as a sacrifice to the gods. Specialists with ropes followed the fighting men in order to bind those who had been thrown down before they could recover consciousness. At the end of a battle, the Aztecs returned home with defeated warriors as captives, who subsequently became victims in the sacrificial ritual.

Brundage describes this ritual as follows:

> At the foot of the ascent the captor delivered his captive over to the priests who then dragged him up by the hair if he did not himself make the ascent. On reaching the level of the summit he was immediately thrown backward over the techcatl, four priests bearing heavily down on the limbs, while the fifth one crushed his throat. The sixth priest struck a powerful blow in the center of the upthrust chest and broke through the sternum. Reaching into the wound he ripped out the still-beating heart and turning, held it skyward for a moment—an offering to the god.

The logic of this Aztec sacrificial ritual was not complex. According to Lopez Austin, "As long as men could offer blood and the hearts of captives taken in combat, the power of the sun god would not decline, and he would continue on his course above the earth." To keep the sun "moving in its course so that darkness should not overwhelm the world forever," Soustell says, it was necessary to "feed it every day with its food, 'the precious water'—that is, with human blood." Sacrifice was a "sacred duty toward the sun and a necessity for the welfare of men. In the absence of sacrifice, the "very life of the world would stop."

The purpose of the life of an Aztec warrior was to capture enemy soldiers in order to feed the sun. When the midwife cut the umbilical cord of a baby boy, she harangued him (Soustell, 1970):

> Dear son, you must understand that your home is not here where you have been born, for you are a warrior. Your mission is to give the sun the blood of enemies to drink and feed Tlaltecuhtli, the earth with their bodies. Your country, your inheritance and your father are in the house of the sun, in the sky.

Just as the Aztec warrior was fated to engage in battle in order to capture warriors for sacrifice, so too were the warriors of other Mexican city-states. Their gods also required nourishment. If an Aztec warrior was captured, he would be sacrificed to the god of the other city-state.

THE FIRST WORLD WAR

Unlike the Aztecs, we in the West do not conceive that sacrifice is the purpose of warfare. Rather, we imagine that wars are fought for "real" reasons or purposes—such as conquest, acquisition of territory, economic gain, defending one's homeland, etc. We understand the death or maiming of soldiers in battle as by-products of the attempt to achieve political objectives. We do not say that wars are initiated in order to produce sacrificial victims. Yet the case study that I now will examine—the First World War—produced more victims in four years than were produced in the entire history of the Aztec Empire.

The First World War took place August 1914 to November 1918 and involved many of the world's nations. Casualties of World War I are estimated at 9 million dead and 30 million wounded or missing. The First World War is famous for the way battles were fought. Each side expected a quick victory, which did not occur. Soon hundreds of miles of trenches were built on the Western Front, with French and British soldiers digging themselves in on one side and German soldiers on the other. Battles occurred when troops got out of their trenches and moved toward the opposing trench, hoping to survive the trip through "No Man's Land," cut through the barbed wire, and break through the enemy line.

One typical British "attack" that occurred during the Battle of the Somme in July 1916 is described as follows in the German regimental diary:

Ten columns of extended line could clearly be discerned. Each advancing column was estimated at more than a thousand men, offering such a target as had never been seen before, or thought possible. Never had the machine-gunners such straightforward work to do nor done it so effectively. They traversed to and fro along the enemy's ranks unceasingly.

In August 1916, German troops counter-attacked. War correspondent Philip Gibbs saw them advance towards the British trenches shoulder to shoulder, "like a solid bar" (Gilbert, 1994). It was "sheer suicide":

I saw our men get their machine-guns into action, and the right side of the living bar frittered away, and then the whole line fell into the scorched grass. Another line followed. The German soldiers were tall men, and did not falter as they came forward. But it seemed to me they walked like men conscious of going to death. They died.

This tactic of assaulting enemy trenches with massive numbers of troops—the central military strategy of the First World War—continued to be employed throughout the war despite the perpetual, endless slaughter that continued to occur and the absence of substantial results. For four years the belligerents on the Western Front hammered at each other in battles that cost millions of men their lives but moved the front line at most a mile or so in either direction.

The Germans attacked Verdun in 1916. During six months more than 23 million shells were fired by the two contending armies, an average of more than 100 shells a minute. Verdun remained in French hands, but the death toll there was 650,000 men. When added to that of the earlier battle of the Somme, this made a five-month death toll of almost a million men. It was an average of more than

6,600 men killed every day, more than 277 every hour, nearly five each minute.

WHY THE PERPETUAL SLAUGHTER?

We're dealing with something extraordinary. Each time I return to study this war, I am stunned and deeply disturbed. What was going on? In the face of enormous numbers of casualties—and the fact that most assaults failed—why did generals continue to employ the futile battle strategy described above? Why did soldiers rarely mutiny or fail to obey orders? Eksteins (1989) poses the question, *"Why did soldiers continued to fight?"*:

> What kept them in the trenches? What made them
> go over the top, in long rows? What sustained them
> in constant confrontation with death? We are talking
> here not of professional armies, but of mass armies,
> of volunteers and conscripts, such as the world has
> not seen before. The incidence of insubordination was
> minuscule in relation to the number of men under
> arms and in view of the conditions they had to brave.

In order to understand the meaning of this war, one must begin by articulating the fundamental *structure of thought*—the foundational idea—out of which everything grew. The First World War built upon the ideology of nationalism. When war was declared in 1914, excited crowds gathered and celebrated in every major city. One million volunteers joined the British army during the first year. War Office recruiting stands were inundated with men persuaded of their duty to fight. Soldiers were cheered on as they rushed off to battle.

Combatants joined the military and entered into battle—and civilians supported their willingness or desire to do so—because they believed it was their duty to fight to defend their nation. What occurred during the First World War grew out of "love of country." Monumental orgies of destruction were undertaken and justified in the name of entities or sacred-objects called France, Germany, England, Russia, Italy, etc.

What are "countries" and why do people get so excited about them? What is the relationship between our attachment to nations, on the one hand, and the willingness to kill, die and bear unendurable suffering on the other? John Lennon asked people to conceive of a world not defined or demarcated by nation-states; to envision human existence in the absence of countries. "Imagine there's no country," Lennon sang, "It isn't hard to do." As it turns out, however, it is extremely difficult for people to imagine life in the absence of countries.

THE BODY AND BLOOD OF THE SOLDIER GIVE RISE TO THE REALITY OF THE NATION

During the course of the First World War, soldiers' bodies were fed into the jaws of battle under the assumption that the "life" of the nation was more significant than the lives of human beings. Individual bodies were sacrificed in the name of the greater glory of the body politic. The First World War represented the acting out of the ideological proposition: "The individual must die so that the nation might live."

In war, the body and blood of the sacrificed soldier give rise to the reality of the nation. Killing and dying substantiate the idea that nations exist. The sound and fury of battle function to convince everyone that something profound and real is occurring. Warfare testifies to the existence of nations. Battle—the bodies of dead and wounded soldiers—anchors belief in material reality—persuading us that countries are more than social constructions. Surely, we reflect, human beings would not—could not—kill and die in the name of nothing.

John Horne (in Coetzee and Shevin-Coetzee, 1995) analyzed the published letters of French soldiers who fought in the war. The theme of many of these letters was the idea of national sacrifice as a source of redemption and renewal for the French nation. Shortly before his death, Robert Dubarle wrote of the glorious privilege of "sacrificing oneself, voluntarily." Contemplating the warriors who had fallen around him, French soldier J. Saleilles wondered whether their "gift of blood" was not the "supernatural source of the renewal of life which must be given to our country." If this were the case, then it would be unacceptable to "wail and lament like pagans in the face of all these dead."

F. Belmont—moved by attending a field mass with 500 soldiers— wrote that the war "at least has a purifying role. It is by sacrifice and suffering that regeneration occurs." A Catholic priest put forth a similar idea: "We await the decisive all-out assault. So many sacrifices! May they help bring the resurrection of a greater, more beautiful and truly Christian France." Pierre-Maurice Massoon, a Catholic academic, wrote in April 1916 that one needed an almost "religious faith in one's country to accept such an immolation without revolt and moral disarray."

Why did people believe that suffering and sacrifice would bring about the regeneration or resurrection of France? What does it mean to say that the renewal of the life of one's nation depends upon the "gift of blood" provided by soldiers? These phrases link the death of the soldier to the survival or more abundant life of one's nation. What logic leads to the belief that a nation benefits by virtue of the death of its soldiers?

When injury or death occurs on the field of battle: that is the moment at which blood contained within the body of the soldier flows out of him and into the body politic. The body and blood of the soldier—at that moment—act to energize or regenerate the nation: to bring it back to life.

Writing in the midst of the war, writer Maurice Barrès (1918a) praised French soldiers dying on a daily basis:

> Oh you young men whose value is so much greater than
> ours! They love life, but even were they dead, France
> will be rebuilt from their souls. The sublime sun of
> youth sinks into the sea and becomes the dawn which
> will hereafter rise again.

Soustell notes that the Aztecs believed that the warrior who died in battle or upon the stone of sacrifice "brought the sun to life" and became a "companion of the sun." The sun was the "reincarnation of a dead warrior."

Barrès' fantasy about the fate of the French soldier is nearly identical to the Aztec fantasy. Like Aztec soldiers who brought the sun to life and became companions to the sun, French soldiers, according to Barrès—the "sublime sun of youth"—would become the "dawn which will rise again."

British political leader David Lloyd George stated (Haste, 1977) that every nation was "profligate" of its manpower" and conducted its war activities as if there were no limit to the number of young men who were fit to be "thrown into the furnace to feed the flames of war." He described the First World War as a perpetual, driving force that "shoveled warm human hearts and bodies by the millions into the furnace" (Gilbert, 1994). Just as the Aztecs believed that the hearts and blood of sacrificial victims were required in order to keep the sun god alive, so during the First World War millions of hearts and bodies were sacrificed in order to preserve the lives of nations.

Infantryman Coningsby Dawson fought in the First World War and published two books during the war (*Carry On*, 1917; *The Glory of the Trenches*, 1918) in which he attempted to convey the experiences and motivations of British soldiers. These men, he said

> In the noble indignation of a great ideal, face a worse
> hell than the most ingenious of fanatics ever planned
> or plotted. Men die scorched like moths in a furnace,
> blown to atoms, gassed, tortured. And again other men

step forward to take their places well knowing what will be their fate. Bodies may die, but the spirit of England grows greater as each new soul speeds upon its way.

What an astonishingly direct expression of the fantasy that supports the ideology of warfare! Although Dawson says that bodies may die, *but* the spirit of England grows greater, what he actually seems to be saying is that bodies may die *therefore* the spirit of England grows greater.

What is suggested by this passage is a mathematical relationship between the number of soldiers that perish in battle and the greatness of one's own nation. One's country is great to the extent that it is able and willing to sacrifice the lives of its soldiers. Willingness to sacrifice one's soldiers testifies to the abundant spirit of one's nation.

WAR AS POTLATCH

In December 1915, Douglas Haig was appointed commander-in-chief of the British Expeditionary Force. The British believed that Haig was someone with the courage and resolve to sustain the heavy losses that would be necessary to break through the German line. On July 1, 1916, after an eight-day artillery bombardment in which 1537 British guns fired 1,723,873 rounds, Haig began the attack at the Somme that was designed to bring victory to the Allies. At 7:30 a.m., whistles blew, and the men went 'over the top'. The generals had ordered troops (carrying up to 80 pounds of equipment) to walk in straight lines across No Man's Land, advancing as though forming a military parade.

British soldiers were slaughtered, torn and ripped apart by the German guns. One German machine-gunner wrote: "They went down in their hundreds. You didn't have to aim, we just fired into them." British casualties on the first day of the Battle of the Somme were 20,000 dead and 40,000 wounded—probably more casualties suffered by any army in any war on any single day.

Despite the disaster, Douglas Haig—from his headquarters in the château at Valvion, 50 miles behind the lines—remained confident. He continued to fight the war using a similar strategy of attack for four months, with the same results. Only on November 18, 1916, as winter set in, did the battle finally grind to a halt. A mere six miles of ground had been taken. The final casualties were: British 415,000, French 195,000, Germans perhaps 600,000.

Although his tactic of persisting in a battle strategy that seemed futile drew criticism, General Douglas Haig retained the title of commander-in-chief until the end of the war in 1918. In spite of the enormous casualties and costs of the battles that he initiated, he received encouragement and support from the King and a substantial part of the British populace.

The following letter written to Haig was found among his papers (De Groot, 1988):

> Illustrious General, the expectation of mankind is upon you—the 'Hungry Haig' as we call you here at home. You shall report 500,000 casualties, but the Soul of the empire will afford them. And you shall break through with the cavalry of England and France for the greatest victory that history has ever known. Drive on, Illustrious General!

This anonymous note was preserved by Haig probably because it echoed his own feelings. This letter and similar messages that he received reinforced his belief that there existed a great mass of people who shared his willingness and determination to pursue victory even at the cost of the lives of hundreds of thousands of men.

The "potlatch" is a festival ceremony—practiced by indigenous peoples of the Pacific Northwest Coast—that has been studied extensively by anthropologists. The word means "to give away" or "a gift." The potlatch served as the means by which aspiring nobles validated their status position by giving away gifts and through the lavish distribution—and sometimes ostentatious destruction—of resources and property.

Citing Gaston Bouthoul, Franco Fornari (1975) suggests that war represents a "voluntary destruction of previously accumulated reserves of human capital," an act performed with the implicit intention to "sacrifice a certain number of lives." He compares warfare to the institution of potlatch: Acts of ostentatious destruction whose aim is to "intimidate the rival and, ultimately, give prestige to the donor or destroyer."

The proud claim made in the letter written to Haig—that the soul of the British Empire can well afford 500,000 casualties—conveys this sense of warfare as a form of potlatch or ostentatious destruction. Prestige is conveyed upon the donor or destroyer—the British Empire—by virtue of its capacity to endure or tolerate hundreds of thousands of casualties. The British Empire is so great and powerful that it can afford to throw away its own men.

The First World War may be understood as an extraordinary, monumental form of potlatch or ostentatious destruction, each nation striving to demonstrate its capacity and willingness to throw away or waste men and materials. The greatness and prestige of each nation would be measured according to the quantity of men and materials that could be thrown away or wasted. The First World War constituted a massive, sacrificial competition.

WARFARE AS TRUTH

Franco Fornari calls war the spectacular establishment of a general human situation whereby "death assumes absolute value." The ideas for which we die are considered to be true, he says, because death becomes a "demonstrative process." Willingness to die in battle shows sincerity. Death in battle testifies to the truth of the ideology for which people fight.

The connection between death and truth grows out of our feeling that surely if someone goes so far as to give their life for an idea, then there must be something to this idea. We find it difficult to conceive that human beings would die for an idea possessing no validity. Surely human beings would not kill people and allow themselves to be killed in the name of nothing.

Dead and mangled bodies on the field of battle imply the existence of some "thing" in the name of which the frenzied activity and destruction—the carnage—has occurred, testifying to the reality of that thing. People imagine that if radical acts of destruction are taking place, then they must be occurring based on something real. Surely if England was merely a social construction, soldiers would not allow themselves to be "scorched, blown to atoms, gassed and tortured." Acts of destruction confer reality on the entity or idea in whose name these acts are undertaken.

British infantryman Coningsby Dawson (1918) tried to explain what kept British soldiers going in the First World War in the face of the horrors that they encountered. One motive that kept them at the front, he said, was a "sense of pride." Yet Dawson perceived that "something else" was essential to the endurance of his British comrades:

> It seems a mad thing to say with reference to fighting men, but that other thing which enables you to meet sacrifice gladly is love. It's the love that helps us to die gladly—love for our cause, our pals, our family, our country. Under the disguise of duty one has to do an awful lot of loving at the Front.

War according to Fornari symbolizes destruction put into the service of the preservation of what men love. Those who make war are driven not by a hate need but by a "love need." Men conceive of war as a "duty toward their love object." What is at stake in war, Fornari says, is not so much the safety of the individual as the safety of the "collective love object." The collective love object for which men die and kill is the nation.

Elaine Scarry (1987) claims that war performs a demonstrative function. The dispute that leads to war initiates a process whereby each side calls into question the legitimacy and thereby "erodes the reality of the other country's issues, beliefs, ideas, and self-conception." Wars are undertaken as each side attempts to reassert that its own constructs are "real" and that "only the other side's constructions are 'creations' (and by extension, 'fictions,' 'lies')." In order to certify the reality of its beliefs, each side brings forward and places before its opponent's eyes and, "more important," the eyes of its own population, "all available sources of substantiation."

According to Scarry, the fundamental characteristic of warfare (as compared with other activities that take the form of a contest) is "injuring." Without the requirement that some people be injured, any number of other kinds of contests could be developed in order to determine a "winner" and a "loser". Wars occur, Scarry argues, not only to determine a winner or loser, but to provide an arena in which injuries can occur. Injuries function to allow "derealized and disembodied beliefs to reconnect with the force and power of the material world."

Wars occur, Scarry suggests, when societies or nations—responding to doubts about the validity of their basic ideologies or belief-systems—are unable to draw upon "benign forms of substantiation" to allay their anxiety about the validity of these ideologies or belief-systems. Scarry describes injury in battle as the

> mining of the ultimate substance, the ultimate source of substantiation, the extraction of the physical basis of reality from its dark hiding place in the body out into the light of day, the making available the precious ore of confirmation, the interior content of human bodies, lungs, arteries, blood, brains, the motherlode that will eventually be reconnected to the winning issue, to which it will lend its radical substance, its compelling, heartsickening reality, until benign forms of substantiation come into being.

When a people begin to acutely doubt the truth of their society's fundamental beliefs, leaders may initiate a war in order to put doubts to rest. Injuries, wounds and deaths suffered in battle function to persuade society members of the truth of their nation's ideology. It is as if war is waged in order to generate the following line of thought: "Look, men still are willing to be mutilated and to die for our beliefs. They must be true!"

According to Scarry, the interior content of a soldier's body— "lungs, arteries, blood and brains" that ooze into the light of day— constitute the "motherlode" that substantiates the issue for which the war is being fought. The content of the wounded soldier's body on the field of battle constitutes the precious "ore of confirmation."

In war, Scarry says, the "incontestable reality of the body"—the body in pain, the body maimed, the body dead and hard to dispose of—is "conferred on an ideology." The ideology thus achieves for a time the force and status of material "fact" by the "sheer weight of the multitudes of damaged and opened human bodies." Warfare, in short, is that cultural activity that seeks to produce dead and wounded soldiers in order to establish the truth of a society's ideology.

THE NATION-STATE KILLS ITS OWN SOLDIERS

During the Aztec period, one Mexican city-state fought other Mexican city-states with the objective of capturing sacrificial victims that became offerings to its gods. Upon returning from one typical battle, Aztec warriors reported to their King, Moeteuzcoma, providing an account of what had transpired. They told him that they had taken a goodly number of captives, but that 370 of their own warriors had died or been lost through capture. Moeteuzcoma replied: "Behold, brothers, how true was the word of the ancestors who taught us that the sun...feeds alike from both sides" (Brundage, 1986).

Conquest—winning or losing—was one dimension of Aztec warfare. However, as Brundage observes, from the god's point of view neither side won or lost. The god could not lose in any case. Whatever the outcome of a war, gods would be fed with the bodies and blood of sacrificial victims.

In the West, we insist that the maiming or death of soldiers (and civilians) in battle represent unfortunate by-products as we wage war in order to achieve other goals. We assume that killing and dying is undertaken in the name of real objectives. Heretofore, we have not considered the possibility that killing and dying constitute the *fundamental purpose* of warfare.

In our conventional way of thinking, a soldier is killed by the enemy. When French or British soldiers got out of trenches during the First World War, ran toward enemy lines and were slaughtered, we say that Germans killed them. When German soldiers got out of trenches and ran toward enemy lines, we say that they were killed by the English or French.

Wouldn't it be more parsimonious to say that French soldiers were killed by the French nation and its leaders—who asked them to get out of trenches and run into artillery shells and machine-gun fire? Wouldn't it be more accurate to state that German soldiers were killed by the German nation and its leaders—who also asked their soldiers to get out of trenches and run into artillery shells and machine-gun fire? We disguise the sacrificial meaning of warfare by delegating the killing of soldiers to the enemy.

In her groundbreaking *Blood Sacrifice and the Nation* (1999), Carolyn Marvin suggests that our deepest secret, the "collective group taboo" is knowledge that society depends on the "death of its own members at the hands of the group." At the behest of the group, Marvin says, the lifeblood of community members must be shed. Marvin calls soldiers the "sacrificial class" to whom we delegate the shedding of blood. The soldier is our chosen victim. When he dies for the country, Marvin says, he dies for all of us.

Gwynne Dyer (1985) cites General John Hackett: "You offer yourself to be slain: This is the essence of being a soldier. By becoming soldiers, men agree to die when we tell them to." Joanna Bourke observes that the most important point to be made about the male body during the First World War was that it was "intended to be mutilated." We represent war as a drive for conquest an outlet for energetic, aggressive activity even as its purpose and inevitable consequence is mutilation and death. We encourage the soldier's delusion of masculine virility and call him a hero—in order to lure him into becoming a sacrificial victim.

PART THREE

THE LOGIC OF
WAR AND GENOCIDE

CHAPTER VI

Dying for the Country

INTRODUCTION

Insofar as human beings have engaged in armed political conflict throughout recorded history, war often is thought of as an immutable cultural institution, even a natural occurrence. In my view, however, the persistence of warfare as a social institution should be interrogated rather than taken for granted. War represents an idea or form of activity created by human beings. We transform war into a problematic by posing the question: "Why?" Why has war been a recurring element of human social life and history? Why have people embraced war in spite of the fact that its consequences invariably are destruction and death?

Hitler was a human being, even if we prefer to think that he was not. We would like to separate Hitler from the human race by pretending he was exceptional; an anomaly. We want to rescue our self-esteem, that is, that part of our self-esteem derived from identification with civilization and belief in the beneficence of society. We prefer to draw a contrast between violence and killing, on the one hand, and civilization on the other, as if these were separate and distinct phenomena.

It would appear, however, that the massive brutality of Hitler's war against the Soviet Union—and the Holocaust—were not separate from the ideals of society, but rather were intimately bound to them. Hitler declared: "We may be inhumane, but if we rescue Germany, we have performed the greatest deed in the world." The violence that Hitler generated grew out of his desire to save Germany by wiping out an enemy whose continued existence, he believed, would result in the destruction of his nation and Western civilization.

War grows out of military institutions that are significant elements of society. People debate about whether particular wars are good or bad, right or wrong, necessary or unnecessary, etc. But most people see the military as a necessary—if perhaps unfortunate—dimension of society. In the darkness of a movie theater, however—witnessing the chaos, mayhem and absurdity of battle—people frequently whisper to themselves, "War is insane."

Genocide like warfare is a collective or societal rather than individual form of violence. Unlike war, however, genocidal behavior usually is viewed as transgressing society's norms; an aberration. Had Hitler simply waged war—and not been responsible for the Holocaust—people today might view him as a failed military leader rather than as a monster, someone like Napoleon who caused the death of millions of people as he failed in his attempt to conquer the world.

Nine million men were killed and over 21 million wounded in the First World War. The Generals who directed the war and were responsible for the deaths of millions—men such as British General Douglas Haig—are sometimes called stupid because of their failed military strategies. Yet rarely are they accused of being mass-murderers, or called evil.

In Hitler's mind, warfare and genocide were not separate phenomena. The Final Solution grew out of Hitler's ideas on the nature of warfare. If society gave him the right to sacrifice his own soldiers, Hitler reflected, why did he not also have the right to destroy the mortal enemy of the German people? The logic of genocide grew out of the logic of war.

WHY DID HITLER WAGE WAR?

People often assume that war has a rational purpose; that it revolves around motives like conquest, territorial expansion, defense of one's nation's borders, the pursuit of economic interests, etc. A standard historical account of the Second World War states that Hitler dreamt of building a "vast German Empire sprawling across Central and Eastern Europe;" that his objective was to wage a war of conquest against the Soviet Union in order to make Germany the "most powerful state in all of Europe."

Based on 40 years of research, I have discovered that there are "hidden narratives" operating beneath the radar of political history. Do we really understand why Hitler waged a war that resulted in the deaths of tens of millions of people and destruction of his own nation? Do we know why he felt it was necessary to kill every single Jew on the face of the earth?

Instead of believing that we know the answers to these questions, I suggest that we begin with the assumption that we do not know the answers. We begin to discern or to understand what Hitler had in mind by listening closely to what he said—by paying attention to the words that he uttered. What Hitler *did* followed closely based on what he *said*.

Hitler declared war on September 1, 1939—as German airplanes and troops crossed the Polish border in a devastating Blitzkrieg. The following passage is from the speech that Hitler delivered to the Reichstag (Snyder, 1961):

> As a National Socialist and a German soldier, I enter upon this fight with a stout heart! My whole life has been but one continuous struggle for my people, and that whole struggle has been inspired by one single conviction: Faith in my people! I ask of every German what I myself am prepared to do at any moment: to be ready to lay down his life for his people and for

his country. If anyone thinks that he can evade this national duty directly or indirectly, he will perish.

Hitler says that he is entering the fight inspired by "faith in his people" and asks every German to do what he was prepared to do: to lay down his life at any moment. Anyone, however, who thought that he could evade this national duty—to lay down one's life—would "perish."

This passage constitutes a prophecy—a prediction of everything that was to follow. The fundamental template for the war—its master plan—was set forth right at the beginning. Hitler states that what will be required in this war is for Germans to sacrifice themselves—to lay down their lives for their country.

On the other hand, Hitler insisted that people who thought they could evade the duty to lay down their lives for the country—would perish. In the Second World War, unlike the First, there would be no shirkers. Hitler's mission in waging war was to try to get *everyone* to die.

IDENTITY OF SELF AND NATION

Nazism asserted an absolute identity between self and nation. Hitler's ideology of *Volksgemeinschaft*—the community of the German people—required overcoming "bourgeois privatism" in order to unconditionally "equate the individual fate with the fate of the nation." The Volk, according to Hitler, encompassed and embraced each and every German. "No one is excepted from the crisis of the Reich," he said. "There may not be a single person who excludes himself from this joint obligation." Nazism insisted that everyone partake of the life of the community. "This Volk," Hitler declared, "is but yourselves."

Nazism revolved around worshipping the German nation. Hitler said: "We do not want to have any other God, only Germany." Hitler was a fanatic preacher, obsessed with his god, imploring and exhorting the German people to devote their lives to the god to which he had devoted his own life:

> Our future is Germany. Our today is Germany. And our past is Germany. Let us take a vow this morning, at every hour, in each day, to think of Germany, of the nation, of our German people. You cannot be unfaithful to something that has given sense and meaning to your life.

Nazism represented negation of individuality in the name of the community. "You are nothing, your nation is everything," Hitler proclaimed. Morality or virtue entailed abandoning one's own desires in the name of the collective. According to Nazi ideology, one could not choose to devote one's life to one's nation or choose not to do so. Rather, renunciation of individual interests in order to devote oneself to the community was a sacred obligation from which no one was exempt.

The ultimate act of self-renunciation was willingness to die for Germany. Reflecting on the loyalty and devotion of his comrades, Hitler observed that more than once, thousands and thousands of young Germans had "stepped forward with self-sacrificing resolve to sacrifice their young lives freely and joyfully on the altar of the beloved fatherland." Hitler glorified the idea of "dying for one's country," building his ideology on this commonplace idea and carrying it through to an extreme, bizarre conclusion.

ARYAN WILLINGNESS FOR SELF-SACRIFICE

We think of National Socialism as the quintessence of brutality and immorality. The Nazis did not see it this way. Goebbels stated that to be a National Socialist meant to "subordinate the I to the Thou, sacrifice the personality for the whole." He defined Nazism (Rhodes, 1980) as "service, renunciation for individuals and a claim for the whole, fanatic of love, courage to sacrifice, resignation for the Volk." A U.S. Department of State booklet (Murphy, 1943) explicated Nazi ideology as a conviction that "consecrates its whole life to the service of an idea, a faith, a task or duty even when it knows that the destruction of its own life is certain."

Goebbels contrasted the creative, constructive philosophy of National Socialism—with its idealistic goals—to the Jewish philosophy of "materialism and individualism." *Hitler's Official Programme* (Feder, 1971) inveighed against leaders of public life who all worshipped the same god, "individualism," and whose sole incentive was "personal interest." The essence of the Nazi complaint against Jews was that they lacked the capacity to sacrifice themselves for the sake of the community.

The popular concept is that the Nazis were intent upon producing a race of supermen. Hitler did believe in the "superiority" of the Aryan race, but his idea of what constituted Aryan superiority is quite different from what is commonly assumed. Further, what made Aryans superior did not necessarily guarantee victory in war. On the contrary, Hitler feared that the Aryan trait that made them superior as culture-builders might lead to the downfall and extinction of the race rather than to its triumph and survival.

According to Hitler's theory propounded in *Mein Kampf*, what was unique about the Aryan was his willingness to abandon self-interest and transcend egoism in the name of surrendering to the community. What was most strongly developed in the Aryan, Hitler said, was the self-sacrificing will to "give one's personal labor and if necessary one's own life for others." The Aryan was not "greatest in his mental abilities as such," but rather in the extent of his willingness to "put all his abilities in the service of the community." The Aryan, according to Hitler, willingly "subordinates his own ego to the life of the community" and "if the hour demands it" even sacrifices himself.

The Jew by contrast, Hitler believed, represented the "mightiest counterpart to the Aryan." Whereas Aryans willingly sacrificed themselves for the community, in the Jewish people the will to self-sacrifice does not go beyond "the individual's naked instinct of self-preservation." The Jew lacked completely, Hitler believed, the most essential requirement for a cultured people, "the idealistic attitude." The Jew's "absolute absence of all sense of sacrifice" expressed itself as "cowardice."

HITLER'S EXPERIENCE OF THE FIRST WORLD WAR

Hitler was one of the 65 million men who fought in the First World War, an instance of mass-slaughter in which 9 million men were killed and nearly 30 million wounded or reported missing. During the period of 1914-1918 across Europe and the wider world, men were killed at an average rate of more than 6000 per day. Like many men who fought in this war, Hitler suffered in the trenches, endured the wet and cold and scarcity of food, the rats and bed-bugs, and the endless artillery barrage. He witnessed the death and dismemberment of hundreds of his comrades and experienced the stench of their decaying bodies.

It is miraculous that Hitler himself was not killed. According to Walter S. Frank's study (2004) of Hitler and the First World War, the chance that a 1914 volunteer in Hitler's regiment would be killed or maimed was almost guaranteed. Because of replacements, Hitler's regiment—that consisted of 3600 men in 1914—suffered 3754 killed before the war ended. Hitler told an English reporter (Frank, 2004) that on one occasion while eating, he moved from one spot in a trench to another 20 yards away. Only a few seconds later, an artillery shell exploded on the very spot from which he had moved, killing every one of his comrades.

One might expect that his trench experiences would have humanized Hitler—sensitized him to the suffering and destruction wrought by war. One would think he would have become highly critical of the leaders of his nation's war effort such as Paul von Hindenburg and Erich Ludendorff, whose military strategies led to the deaths of 2 million German soldiers. Yet astonishingly, Hitler rarely complained or expressed regrets about what he had gone through. Nor did he cease to admire and support Germany's military leaders.

WILLINGNESS TO DIE FOR ONE'S COUNTRY

Why did Hitler's experiences not lead him to critique the ideology of warfare? More broadly, why are human beings unable to abandon war, which is the source of profound suffering, degradation and death? The problem is the relationship between the ideology of warfare and attachment to one's nation. War is waged in the name of a sacred ideal from which people refuse to separate: one's beloved country.

Hitler wrote in *Mein Kampf*: "When in the long war years Death snatched so many a dear comrade and friend from our ranks, it would have seemed to me almost a sin to complain. After all, were they not dying for Germany?" Hitler refused to complain about the death of his comrades in battle—felt that it was a "sin" to do so— because they had *died for Germany*. One's own nation represents an absolute that allows and justifies anything and everything.

Hitler asserted that any man who loves his people proves it "solely by the sacrifices which he is prepared to make for it." He stated that National Socialism meant acting with a "boundless and all-embracing love for the people," and if necessary "to die for it." Giving one's life for the community, he proclaimed, constituted the "crown of all sacrifice." Within the framework of Hitler's radical nationalism, in short, dying for one's country represented the apogee of love and devotion. Nazism was an ideology of martyrdom revolving around "laying down one's life for one's people and country."

Hitler glorified war and the death of the German soldier in battle. In *Mein Kampf*, he wrote that in 1914 his young volunteer regiment had received its baptism of fire. With "Fatherland love in our heart and songs on our lips," Hitler said, his young regiment had "gone into the battle as to a dance." The most precious blood there sacrificed itself joyfully, in the faith that it was "preserving the independence and freedom of the fatherland."

In July 1917, Hitler reports, his regiment set foot for the second time on the ground that was "sacred to all of us." This ground was sacred because in it the best comrades "slumbered." Most of them were "still almost children" who had run to their deaths with "gleaming eyes for the one true fatherland." Hitler and his fellow soldiers stood with respectful emotion at this shrine of "loyalty and obedience to the death."

WHY DO THE BEST HUMAN BEINGS DIE IN WAR WHILE THE WORST SURVIVE?

This is not to say that questions and doubts had not arisen in the mind of Hitler and other Germans after their nation's defeat in the First World War. In *Mein Kampf,* Hitler conveyed his feelings and reflections upon learning that Germany had surrendered and signed the armistice:

> And so it had all been in vain. In vain all the sacrifices and privations; in vain the hunger and thirst of months which were often endless; in vain the hours in which, with mortal fear clutching at our hearts, we nevertheless did our duty; and in vain the death of the two millions who died. Was this the meaning of the sacrifice which the German mother made to the fatherland when with sore heart she let her best-loved boys march off, never to see them again?

What had been the purpose of the war? Why had 2 million German soldiers been killed and 4 million wounded? What had been the meaning of the monumental sacrifices? These questions cried out for an answer.

Hitler responded to questions about the meaning of German sacrifices by deflecting it into another one. The question, "Why had Germans soldiers died?" transmogrified into the question: "Why had German soldiers died while other Germans had not died?" Hitler observed that for each "Hero who had made the supreme sacrifice" there was a "shirker who cunningly dodged death." Hitler became obsessed with the idea that while many men had died, some had avoided fighting altogether. Contemplating the idea that many had sacrificed their lives while others had not, Hitler became deeply disturbed and enraged.

We have noted that Hitler judged the worth of a human being based on this human being's capacity and willingness to sacrifice for the community. He stated that during the First World War, one extreme of the population, which was constituted of the best elements, had given a typical example of its heroism and had "sacrificed itself almost to a man." Whereas the other extreme, which was constituted of the worst elements of the population, had "preserved itself almost intact." While for four-and-a-half years the best human material was being "thinned to an exceptional degree on the battlefields," the worst material "wonderfully succeeded in saving themselves."

Thus a conundrum arose that would preoccupy Hitler for the rest of his life: Why in war do the best human beings die while the worst survive? Our ordinary expectation is that if we perform in accordance with morality or virtue, we will be rewarded; whereas if we act immorally, we will be punished. Hitler discovered that what occurs in war is the opposite of what we feel should occur. In war, those who adhere to societal norms by enthusiastically performing their duty are killed. While those who behave immorally—by evading their social responsibility to fight for their country—are rewarded by survival. Hitler was alarmed and agitated by this profound unfairness or injustice.

JEWISH "SHIRKERS"

Upon returning home from the front, Hitler reports in *Mein Kampf* that what he discovered was that all of the offices were "filled with Jews." He claimed that "nearly every clerk was a Jew and nearly every Jew was a clerk." Hitler was amazed at this plethora of "warriors of the chosen people" and could not help compare them with their "rare representatives at the front." Thus, the question of why some had died in the war and others had not—why the best had been killed while the worst survived—mutated into the question: "Why, while German soldiers were dying at the front, were Jews safe, comfortable and secure at home?"

Hitler claimed that during the time German soldiers were fighting the war, Jews at home—men who had avoided joining the army—fomented revolution and took over the government. He became filled with fantasies of revenge, putting forth an enigmatic idea linking the death of German soldiers at the front with the murder of Jews. In *Mein Kampf,* Hitler said: "If the best men were dying at the front, the least we could do was to wipe out the vermin."

He declared that if at the beginning of the War and during the War "twelve or fifteen thousand of these Hebrew corrupters of the people had been held under poison gas," as happened to hundreds of thousands of German soldiers, then the sacrifice of millions at the front "would not have been in vain." It would appear that Hitler tried to come to terms with the First World War by suggesting that the death of millions of Germany's soldiers would become bearable only if Jews too were compelled to die.

Hitler's vision of war and genocide constituted an ideology of death insisting that no one should be exempt from the obligation to sacrifice one's life for the national community. The Holocaust grew directly out of Hitler's experience of the First World War. Hitler and his comrades had been subjected to poison gas in the trenches during that war. In the spirit of "Do unto others as has been done unto you," Hitler would subject Jews to poison gas during the Second War.

The Holocaust expressed Hitler's idea that no one should be allowed to escape or evade the obligation to sacrifice one's life for Germany. Hitler believed that the best human beings had been killed in the First World War while the worst had survived. In the Second World War, the worst human beings would not be spared. Just as German soldiers were required to give over their bodies and lives to the nation-state, so Jews also would be required to do so.

AS GERMAN SOLDIERS DIE, SO MUST JEWS

Hitler joined the army in 1914 at the behest of his nation and its leaders. By 1939—25 years later—he was Germany's leader. Now it was his turn to declare war and to ask young men to enter the battle-field. Hitler's familiarity with war did not deter him. He knew that Germany's soldiers would die and be maimed. However, now that he was commander-in-chief, why should he waver? Had the German leadership hesitated to declare war in 1914 and to send young German men to die at the front? Was a soldier not obligated to do his duty: to enter into battle when asked to do so, and if necessary to make the 'supreme sacrifice'?

As the attack against Russia began, German General Gerd von Rundstedt in an article entitled "Sacrifice for Germany" (Baird, 1974) admonished the soldier of the Second World War to emulate the examples of his brothers in the First World War and "to die in the same way, to be as strong, unswerving and obedient, to go happily and as a matter of course to his death." As war on the Eastern Front progressed, Goebbels was satisfied to note that "The German soldiers go into battle with devotion, like congregations going into service." German soldiers did not rebel against the duty to fight and die. They went like sheep to the slaughter.

The Final Solution or systematic extermination of the Jewish people began before the construction of death camps and gas chambers. As the German army moved eastward into the Soviet Union in late 1941 and early 1942, they were followed by the

Einsatzgruppen or mobile killing units. Approximately 1.5 million Jews were shot and killed, many of them buried in gorges that bear a striking resemblance to the trenches of the First World War.

Hitler professed to be undisturbed by the extermination of men, women, and children, providing the following rationale: "If I don't mind sending the pick of the German people into the hell of war without regret for the shedding of valuable German blood, then I have naturally the right to destroy millions of men of inferior races who increase like vermin" (Meltzer, 1976). Here we approach the crux of the matter and meaning of the Holocaust.

Hitler appears to be saying that if he had no compunctions about sending German soldiers to die in battle, then why should he have compunctions about sending Jews—mortal enemies of the German people—to their deaths? The logic of genocide derived from the logic of war. Hitler declared that if German soldiers had to die, so too must Jews. No one was exempt. Everyone had to die for Germany.

What disturbed Hitler about the First World War was that some had died, whereas others had not. The best men had been killed, while the worst men survived. Hitler was enraged when contemplating the idea that many Germans had sacrificed their lives, while others—shirkers, war deserters, and Jews—had avoided fighting entirely. In the Second World War, things would be different. This time, Hitler insisted, everyone would participate equally. Jews also would have to lay down their lives.

Ronald Hayman in his biographical study of Hitler (*Hitler and Geli*, 1997) reports an encounter between Hitler and his friend Henny von Schirach. She had returned to Germany in April 1943 after visiting friends in occupied Amsterdam and became aware that helpless women were being taken away and transported to camps. After dinner at Obersalzberg, Hitler turned to his friend and said "You've come from Holland?" She replied, "Yes, that's why I'm here, I wanted to talk to you. I've seen frightful things. I can't believe that's what you want."

"You're sentimental, Frau von Schirach," Hitler replied. Then he jumped to his feet and formed with his hands two bowls, which he moved up and down like scales as he said loudly and insistently:

> Look—every day ten thousand of my most valuable men are killed, men who are irreplaceable, the best. The balance is wrong; the equilibrium in Europe has been upset. Because the others aren't being killed: they survive, the ones in camps, the inferior ones. So what's it going to look like in Europe in a hundred years? In a thousand?

Hitler undertook the extermination of the Jewish people, it would appear, in order to balance the scale of death. As the best human beings—German soldiers—were dying in vast numbers on the field of battle, so it would be necessary to make certain that the worst human beings—Jews—died as well.

Members of the Aryan race—loyal and obedient—willingly sacrificed their lives. The German soldier, as General von Rundstedt put it, would go "happily and as a matter of course to his death." He would be prepared at any moment as Hitler stated in his declaration of war to "lay down his life for his people and his country." Jews on the other hand, according to Hitler, were a race incapable or unwilling to sacrifice for the community. In the case of Jews, it was necessary that they be compelled to die.

SACRIFICIAL DEATH STRIPPED OF HONOR

The Second World War and Holocaust were two sides of the same coin. War provided the occasion for Hitler to sacrifice his own people. Once again the German soldier would demonstrate "loyalty and obedience unto death." The Holocaust represented another form of sacrifice or "dying for the country." The norms of war define soldiers—one's own and the enemy's—as the class of people that must fight in battle and—if necessary—die. Genocide represented an extension and expansion of the logic of warfare, enlarging the pool of sacrificial victims.

We speak of Hitler's extermination of the Jews as the Holocaust. This word derives from the word *olah* in the Hebrew Bible, which has the religious meaning of a burnt-sacrifice. In the Greek translation of the Old Testament the word became *holokauston*, an "offering wholly consumed by fire" (Meltzer, 1976). What Hitler did added another meaning to the dictionary definition: "A complete or thorough sacrifice or destruction, especially by fire, as of large number of human beings."

Use of the term Holocaust to describe what happened suggests we understand that the extermination of the Jews was a form of sacrifice. However, we hesitate to articulate the precise meaning of this sacrifice. Perhaps we do not wish to acknowledge that—with regard to the fate of the Jewish people—Hitler accomplished what he set out to achieve. He sacrificed Jews to the god that he worshipped, Germany.

In the First World War, German soldiers died in massive numbers. Hitler believed that Jews had acted deviously in order to avoid fighting and dying. In the Second World War, German soldiers again would be expected to "lay down their lives for their people and country." In this Second World War, however, unlike during the First, Jews would not be allowed to be "shirkers".

Hitler had stated in his Declaration of War that if anyone thought that he could "evade the national duty" (to lay down one's life for the country), that person would "perish." The Final Solution was undertaken in order to make certain that Jews—like German soldiers—would perish. They too would be required to hand their bodies over to Hitler and Germany—and to die.

The Holocaust reveals the abject and degrading fate of a body that has been given over to—taken over by—the state. A soldier is required to enter into battle at the behest of his nation, often dying a brutal, ugly and horrific death. However, in spite of the brutality and ugliness of his death, the soldier's sacrifice—dying for his country—frequently is viewed as noble and beautiful.

It is impossible, however, to view the death of a Jew in the gas chamber as noble and beautiful. The Holocaust depicts the ugliness, futility and meaninglessness of submission to the nation-state: sacrificial death stripped of words such as honor, heroism and glory.

CHAPTER VII

The Logic of Mass Murder

INTRODUCTION

The Nazis called it the "Final Solution to the Jewish problem." We now refer to this event as the Holocaust. Whatever one calls it, the systematic murder of 6 million Jews was one of the most horrific events in history. It is difficult to comprehend why a seemingly civilized nation would—with brutal determination—kill millions of people simply because they were members of a particular religious or racial group.

Since the Second World War ended in 1945, thousands of books have been written about Hitler, National Socialism, and the Holocaust. We are beginning to understand how and why the Final Solution came into being. I wish to propose a "solution" to the problem or puzzle of the Holocaust: to provide an explanation. I will attempt to articulate Hitler's mindset: to reveal what Hitler was thinking when he decided to exterminate the Jewish race.

In 1933, the population of Germany was 66 million. There were 550,000 Jews in Germany at that time, which meant that Jews constituted less than one percent of the population. The Jewish people posed no threat to Germany. Nonetheless, Hitler experienced Jews as a profound threat—and decided that the Jewish race had to be destroyed. By what logic did Hitler conclude that Germany had to exterminate the Jewish people?

Hitler believed that the essence of morality lay in the willingness of an individual to sacrifice his life for the community. He defined nationalism as the willingness to act with a "boundless and all-embracing love for the people and, if necessary, to die for it." Hitler wrote in *Mein Kampf* that in the First World War thousands and thousands of young Germans had stepped forward with self-sacrificing resolve to "sacrifice their young lives freely and joyfully at the altar of the fatherland."

According to Hitler's theory propounded in *Mein Kampf,* what was unique about the Aryan was his willingness to abandon self-interest and transcend egoism in the name of surrendering to the community. What was most strongly developed in the Aryan, Hitler said, was the self-sacrificing will to "give one's personal labor and if necessary one's own life for others." The Aryan according to Hitler willingly subordinates his own ego to the life of the community and "if the hour demands it even sacrifices himself."

The Jew by contrast, Hitler claimed, represented the "mightiest counterpart to the Aryan." Whereas the Aryan willingly sacrificed himself for the community, in the Jewish people the will to self-sacrifice did not go beyond the individual's "naked instinct of self-preservation." The Jew lacked completely, Hitler said, the most essential requirement for a cultured people, the "idealistic attitude." The Jew's "absolute absence of all sense of sacrifice" manifest itself as "cowardice."

Hitler's theory about the sacrificial willingness of Aryans and sacrificial unwillingness of Jews grew out of his experience of the First World War. Hitler claimed that while German men had died in great numbers, Jews survived because they avoided military duty. Hitler identified Jews as "shirkers" who refused to go into battle: to sacrifice for Germany.

Historical studies show that German-Jewish men died in the First World War in the same proportion as other German men. Nonetheless, Hitler fanatically embraced and promulgated his theory that Jewish men had not sacrificed their lives during the First World War. He became enraged contemplating the idea that some men had sacrificed their lives during the First World War, while others had escaped military duty.

Believing that Jews had shirked their duty to fight and die in the First World War, Hitler was determined that things would be different in the Second World War. Again, German soldiers would be required to die in battle. This time, however, Jews too would be compelled to forfeit their lives. They too would be obligated to submit—to give their bodies over—to the German nation-state.

THE FIRST WORLD WAR

The First World War—like the Holocaust—was an instance of mass slaughter generated by nation-states. The war began in 1914 and ended in 1918—23 years before the beginning of the Holocaust. Hitler was among 65 million men who fought in this war—truly a world war involving over 100 countries. Nine million men were killed. Casualties (dead, injured and missing in action) are estimated at 37 million.

The war was fought by Germany on the Eastern Front against Russia and on the Western Front against France, Great Britain and the United States. By the end of the war in November 1918, 11 million German soldiers had been mobilized. It is estimated that 2 million Germans were killed; 4 million were injured and over 1 million reported missing in action. For Germany, the First World War was a catastrophe.

Hitler fought in the war for four years—from its inception in 1914 to 1918. Although most of the troops in his regiment were killed, Hitler miraculously survived. Near the end of the war, he was injured in a poison-gas attack and temporarily blinded. He was lying in a hospital bed recovering when—in November 1918—he learned that Germany had surrendered.

Hitler deeply identified with the German cause and experienced Germany's defeat as a traumatic blow. He claimed in *Mein Kampf* that upon learning that Germany had surrendered, he wept for the first time since the death of his mother. Hitler never accepted the fact of Germany's loss. He felt that had the war continued, Germany would have emerged victorious. He blamed Germany's defeat on the Social Democratic government that took power upon the abdication of Kaiser Wilhelm.

Determined to avenge Germany's defeat, Hitler entered politics. He became leader of the National Socialist party—and Chancellor of Germany in 1934. The Second World War began when Germany attacked Poland on September 1, 1939—nearly 21 years after Germany had been defeated in the First World War. For Hitler, the Second World War was a continuation of the First. He was determined that—this time—Germany would not surrender.

The First World War is remembered not only for the massive number of casualties suffered, but for the strange way in which battles were fought. After a few months of fighting that produced no decisive results, troops dug miles and miles of trenches north to south in France. British and French troops settled down in trenches on the western side, while German troops settled into trenches on the eastern side. The two lines of trenches sometimes were separated by distances of only 100-300 yards.

A typical battle occurred when soldiers on one side got out of their trench and moved forward to attack the opposing trench. The attacking troops hoped to survive the artillery shelling and machine-gun fire that they encountered, cut through the barbed wire protecting the enemy trench, and break through the enemy line.

Attackers moved forward usually without seeking cover—and were mowed down by machine-gun bullets and artillery shells before reaching the enemy's trench. In the following passage (Eksteins 1989), a German machine-gunner describes the British attack at the Somme that occurred on July 1, 1916:

We were surprised to see them walking. Officers went
in front. One of them was walking calmly, carrying a
walking stick. We started firing. We just had to load
and reload. They went down in the hundreds. We didn't
have to aim. We just fired into them.

In another battle, the British attacked Loos in 1915. British troops
crossed a road and approached the German line. Their numerical
superiority was considerable, but several dozen machine-guns faced
them. The German regimental diary describes what happened:

Ten columns advanced, each column with more than
a thousand men offering such a target as had never
been seen before. Never had the machine-gunners such
straightforward work to do nor done it so effectively.
The machine-gunners stood and fired triumphantly
into the mass of men advancing across open grassland.
The enemy infantry could be seen falling literally in
hundreds.

A similar method of attack—with similarly disastrous results—
was used by the French and Germans. In spite of its futility, this
battle strategy continued to be employed day after day, month after
month, year after year. After four years and hundreds of battles, little
had changed and nothing had been accomplished from a military
or political standpoint—apart from the fact that now millions of
young men were dead or maimed.

What was going on? Why did generals continue to employ a
battle strategy that consisted of asking soldiers to get out of trenches
and to run into machine-gun fire and artillery shelling? Why were
young men being sent to die so promiscuously? To this day, historians cannot adequately explain the endless carnage of the First
World War.

I began to study this war after having researched the Holocaust
for over 20 years. My initial reaction upon reading about the First

World War was similar to the reaction of some people when they first learn about the Holocaust: incomprehensible. Why were "civilized" nations such as France, Great Britain and Germany acting to murder their own people?

The British initiated the Battle of the Somme on July 1, 1916, desperately hoping to break through the German lines. They failed miserably. British casualties were 60,000 on the first day, with over 20,000 soldiers killed—most in the first hour of the attack. Historian John Keegan (1976) compares British soldiers at the Battle of the Somme to Jewish Holocaust victims, describing the "long docile lines of young men, shoddily uniformed, heavily burdened, plodding forward across a featureless landscape to their own extermination inside the barbed wire."

HITLER AND THE FIRST WORLD WAR

Hitler was among millions of men who fought in the First World War. He suffered in the trenches, endured the wet and cold and mud, scarcity of food, rats and bedbugs, and the endless artillery barrages that reigned down upon men huddled in holes beneath the ground. Hitler witnessed the death and dismemberment of hundreds of his comrades—and experienced the stench of their decaying bodies. Over 4,000 men in his regiment were killed, but Hitler survived. He was a dedicated and decorated soldier. On August 4, 1918, Hitler was awarded the Iron Cross, First Class.

As I've noted, Hitler experienced his nation's defeat as a profound trauma. He reflected on Germany's loss of the war in *Mein Kampf*:

> And so it had all been in vain. In vain all the sacrifices and privations; in vain the hunger and thirst of months which were often endless; in vain the hours in which with mortal fear clutching at our hearts, we nevertheless did our duty; and in vain the death of the two millions

who died. Was this the meaning of the sacrifice which the German mother made to the fatherland when with sore heart she let her best-loved boys march off, never to see them again?

What had been the purpose and meaning of the monumental sacrifices made by German soldiers and the German people? Over 2 million soldiers had died and well over 4 million were wounded. People at home were starving. Women suffered from the absence or loss of husbands; children from the absence or loss of a father.

The quantity of suffering was matched by the horrific experience of war. One German soldier wrote about the rotting bodies of men who had been killed (Whalen, 1984):

Hair fell in clumps from skulls like rotting leaves. Flesh fell from bones like reddish-brown gelatin. In humid nights, cadavers awoke to ghastly life as gas, sputtering, escaped from wounds. The worst was masses of countless worms oozing from corpses.

Hitler must have observed disgusting sights like these hundreds of times. Having witnessed the hideous nature of war—its loathsomeness—up close, one might have expected Hitler to become a pacifist. At least he might have condemned Germany for the slaughter. Or he could have criticized German Generals Erich Ludendorff and Paul von Hindenburg—whose military leadership and strategies led to millions of casualties and the loss of the war.

Hitler did blame and condemn the German parliamentary government (controlled, he claimed, by Jews) for the loss of the war. Because of these "misleaders of the people," he wrote in *Mein Kampf,* the nation had lost millions of crippled and dead. Nevertheless, Hitler continued to idealize warfare and the German nation that had waged war. He did not condemn his country.

Rather, he persisted in glorifying the idea of sacrificial death. In *Mein Kampf,* Hitler asserted that the most "precious German blood" during the First World War had sacrificed itself "joyfully." Though "death snatched so many dear comrades and friends from our ranks," Hitler explained, nevertheless it would have seemed to him a "sin to complain" because—after all—were they not "dying for Germany?"

In spite of the horrors that he had experienced and witnessed— and the tragic results of the war for the German people—Hitler refused to complain. He could not bear to perform a critique of his beloved nation. He could not abandon the idea of warfare because he would not abandon his attachment to "Germany."

Nevertheless, we may assume that Hitler continued to be disturbed by the horrible things he had experienced and witnessed during the First World War. A close reading of *Mein Kampf* reveals how Hitler responded to his wartime experience. An extraordinary psychological shift occurred. This shift—the source of everything that followed—contained the seeds of the Holocaust.

Instead of expressing revulsion—and blaming Germany and its leaders for what had occurred—Hitler tried to deal with doubt and ambivalence by deflecting his psychic energy into another issue. He posed the question: Why during the First World War had some men died—sacrificed their lives—while others had not? More precisely: Why during the First World War had the best young men died while the worst had survived?

Writing in *Mein Kampf* about the First World War, Hitler claimed that while the "best human material was being thinned on battlefields," the worst people "wonderfully succeeded in saving themselves." For each German hero who made the "supreme sacrifice," Hitler said, there was a shirker who "cunningly dodged death" on the pretense of being engaged in "business at home."

Hitler described the German soldiers who died in the First World War—the "best elements of the population"—as heroes who had "sacrificed themselves almost to a man." Those who survived, according to Hitler, were the "worst elements of the population": men who had preserved themselves by "taking advantage of absurd laws."

Hitler thus avoided or evaded the question of why so many German men had died in the First World War. Instead, he focused on the question: "Why had some men died during the First World War whereas other men had not died?" More specifically: "Why had the best men died during the First World War while the worst had survived?"

The best men in Hitler's view were those who volunteered for military service and willingly went into battle. Such men—of course—were more likely to be killed. The worst men, Hitler said, were those who avoided military service and shirked their duty to go into battle. These men naturally were less likely to be killed. Hitler was deeply disturbed by this unfairness.

Although Jewish German soldiers died in the First World War in the same proportion as non-Jewish German soldiers, Hitler nevertheless accused Jewish men of having shirked their duty to fight. He claimed in *Mein Kampf* that upon returning home from the frontline he discovered that the offices were "filled with Jews." According to Hitler, "nearly every clerk was a Jew and nearly every Jew a clerk." Hitler was amazed at this "plethora of warriors of the chosen people" at home and could not help comparing them with their "rare representatives at the front."

Hitler's question—why had the best men died in the First World War while the worst men had survived—thus mutated into the question: "Why had German men died in the First World War while Jewish men had not died? Why were German soldiers suffering at the Front while Jews were safe and comfortable at home?"

Contemplating the idea that Jews had acted to escape or evade their sacrificial obligation during the First World War, Hitler became enraged. Why should German soldiers be dying and not Jews? If the best men were dying at the front, Hitler wrote in *Mein Kampf*, "The least we could do was to wipe out the vermin."

In late 1941, Hitler would exact revenge. Once again, the best men—German soldiers—were dying in battles. This was to be expected. This time, however, Jews would not be allowed to shirk the sacrificial obligation. As German soldiers were dying, so Jews would be compelled to die. Hitler created the Final Solution in order to make certain that they too would "die for Germany."

THE EUTHANASIA PROGRAM

In their 1920 book—*Permission for the Destruction of Life Unworthy of Life*—lawyer Alfred Hoche and psychiatrist Karl Binding proposed that the state consider killing mental patients—people who, they said, were barely human beings and could not contribute to society. The authors posed the question: "Why should the state spend valuable resources maintaining mental hospitals in order to preserve the lives of people who are fundamentally 'useless'?"

The ideas of Hoche and Binding—developed by German scholars, scientists and doctors—were put into practice when the Nazis took power. The "Euthanasia Program" began in 1939 with the killing of defective children (Lifton, 1986). According to a Directive of August 18, 1939, Hitler authorized doctors to consider euthanasia for children under three in whom "serious hereditary diseases were suspected," including mental retardation, mongolism and congenital malformations of all kinds. This was the first instance of Nazi mass-murder.

The next step of the Euthanasia Program extended the killing of children to the killing of the adult mentally ill (Lifton, 1986). Hitler enunciated a "Fuehrer decree" in October 1939, charging Reich leaders with responsibility for "expanding the authority of physicians to the end that patients considered incurable according to the best available human judgment of their state of health can be granted a mercy death." Killing mental patients involved the entire German psychiatric community.

The decision to kill or not to kill was in the hands of physicians, who studied records, examined patients, and filled out forms. If two of three doctors agreed on a diagnosis of "incurable," the patient was selected for "special treatment." Killing was the personal responsibility of the physician and was accomplished through fatal injections, druggings, and starvation—eventually giving way to the more "humane" treatment of killing by carbon monoxide gas. By August 1941—according to meticulously kept records—70,272 patients had been killed.

Selections took place in hospitals. Scholars agree that while Hitler gave the "OK," the program was developed by physicians—and executed voluntarily and enthusiastically. The procedure became quite ordinary. Hospital personnel were not squeamish. In 1941, the psychiatric institution Hadamar celebrated the cremation of the 10,000th mental patient in a special ceremony. Psychiatrists, nurses, and secretaries attended and everyone received a bottle of beer for the occasion (Procter, 1988).

Eventually the killing of mental patients was extended into concentration camps. This was the crucial bridge between the Euthanasia Program and the Final Solution. Several passages from *Permission for the Destruction of Life Unworthy of Life* are cited again and again by scholars tracing the evolution of Nazi mass murder. Hoche and Binding pose the question: "Are there humans who have lost their human characteristics to such an extent that their continued existence has lost all value both for themselves and for society?"

The authors state that those who assess the value of individual lives to the community are painfully aware of "how wasteful we are with the most valuable and self-sufficient lives—full of energy and vigor—and what labor, patience and resources are squandered simply to try to sustain worthless lives." The following passage (see Noakes & Pridham, 2001) is crucial:

> If one thinks of a battlefield covered with thousands of young corpses and compares them with our institutions for idiots—with the care devoted to their inmates—one is deeply shocked by the discrepancy between the sacrifice of man's most precious resource and the tremendous care devoted to creatures that are completely worthless.

Why is the state unconcerned with the lives of its most valuable citizens—soldiers—yet devotes so much care to the lives of its least valuable citizens—idiots and inmates of mental hospitals? This question posed by Hoche and Binding is not unlike the question posed by Hitler in *Mein Kampf*: "Why are the nation's best people—German soldiers—so promiscuously sacrificed in battle, while its worst people—shirkers and war deserters—are allowed to survive?"

In his article "Healing by Killing" (2006), Dr. Sheldon Rubenfeld reports that Alfred Hoche—one of the authors of *Permission for the Destruction of Life Unworthy of Life* —lost his first and only son in the First World War. Hoche used this to argue that if healthy people can make such sacrifices, then why should sick and inferior people not make similar sacrifices?

One may suggest that Hoche and Binding's treatise—like *Mein Kampf*—represented a response to the German experience of the First World War—the trauma of mass death. Like Hitler, these authors sought to comprehend the meaning of the slaughter that had occurred; to understand why the German state had sacrificed the lives of so many young men.

Hoche and Binding, however—like Hitler—are unable to renounce the idea or ideology of warfare. They are unable to condemn the German nation or to hold its leaders accountable for the slaughter that occurred. Rather, Hoche and Binding perform a critique obliquely by commenting upon the discrepancy between how the state treats soldiers and how the state treats mental patients.

Anyone who witnessed a First World War battlefield—"covered with thousands of young corpses"—could observe how wasteful Germany was with its "most valuable and self-sufficient lives—full of energy and vigor." On the other hand, anyone who spent time in one of Germany's mental hospitals could observe how so many resources and so much energy were devoted to sustaining "worthless lives." Why was Germany so reckless with its "most precious resource", while dedicating tremendous care to creatures that were "completely worthless."

The Euthanasia Program—the starting point for Nazi mass murder—would appear to have grown out of ideas like these put forth by Hoche and Binding as well as other German scholars. The reasoning is as follows: if the nation-state can sacrifice (kill) its most valuable citizens—soldiers—should it not also have the right to sacrifice (kill) citizens who make no useful contribution to society—for example, incurable mental patients?

OBEDIENCE (UNTO DEATH)

The most important organizations in Nazi Germany took an oath of absolute allegiance to Hitler. When boys entered Hitler Youth at age 10 they swore: "I will devote all my strength to the savior of our country, Adolf Hitler. I am willing and ready to give up my life for him, so help me God." Upon entering the army, German soldiers vowed: "I swear this sacred oath by God that I will render absolute obedience to the Fuehrer of the German Reich and people, Adolf Hitler, and will be prepared as a courageous soldier to offer my life at any time."

The oath of the SS-man went as follows: "I swear to you, Adolf Hitler, loyalty and bravery. I vow to you and to those you have named to command me, obedience unto death, so help me God." According to an SS manual, every SS-man had to be prepared to "carry out blindly every order issued by the Fuehrer or given by his superior, irrespective of the heaviest sacrifices involved."

German Soldiers and SS-men have been viewed as the epitome of masculine aggression and virility. In reality, the state-of-being of the German soldier and SS-man was precisely the opposite: These men were compelled to submit absolutely—to become slaves for Hitler and Himmler. The condition of the German soldier and SS-man actually was worse than that of a slave. These men were required to die when the Nazi leadership asked them to do so.

HITLER GOES TO WAR

Hitler became Chancellor of Germany in 1934 after a long struggle to achieve power and immediately began thinking about—gearing up for—war. This seemed the natural thing to do. Germany's leaders had sent Hitler and his comrades into battle when he was a young man. Now he was Germany's leader. It was his turn to send young men into battle.

There was no reason for Germany to go to war. After Hitler had been in power for several years, the nation had begun to revive. The economy was doing well. Political strife had diminished. It seemed that Hitler had achieved his goal of uniting the German people and resurrecting his nation.

However, Germany's loss of the First World War still weighed heavily upon Hitler. Further, he experienced Soviet communism as a mortal threat. If Europe was infected with the disease of communism, Hitler believed that this would spell the downfall of Western civilization. Hitler felt he had no other choice. He could not help himself. He felt compelled to take Germany into war.

In conversations with Hermann Rauschning in the mid-Thirties (1940), Hitler discussed the war he eventually would wage. He said that when the time was ripe, he would be prepared for the "blood sacrifice of another young German generation." Hitler declared that he would not hesitate to take the deaths of 2 or 3 million German soldiers on his conscience, "fully aware of the heaviness of sacrifice."

Few had criticized German Generals Erich Ludendorff and Paul von Hindenburg—though their leadership in the First World War led to Germany's defeat and the death of 2 million German soldiers. Indeed, after the war these two generals became national heroes. Von Hindenburg was elected second President of the Weimar Republic in 1925 and re-elected in 1932. Hitler knew that these Generals had sacrificed the lives of millions of young Germans, yet still were idolized. Why then should Hitler have compunctions about waging war and sending millions of young Germans into battle? Was he not commander-in-chief of the army? Why should he—leader of a great nation—hesitate to take Germany into war?

Hitler stated that it was his duty to wage war "regardless of losses." He declared (Rauschning, 1940): "We all know what world war means. We must shake off all sentimentality and be hard. Some day when I go to war I shall not hesitate because of ten million young men I shall be sending to their deaths." Hitler was preparing for the slaughter of German soldiers.

THE EXPLANATION

Having participated in the First World War, Hitler had experienced the horrors of battle and witnessed the death and dismemberment of hundreds of his comrades. Yet he was unable to renounce warfare—to say that war is disgusting and loathsome. Rather, he continued to idealize and glorify warfare. In *Mein Kampf* Hitler declared: "Any man who loves his people proves it solely by the sacrifices which he is prepared to make for it."

Unwilling to condemn the German nation and its leaders for what had occurred during the First World War, Hitler instead focused upon another issue. He became obsessed with the question: "Why had some men died in the First World War—sacrificed their lives—while others had not?" Hitler became enraged when contemplating the idea of "shirkers"— people who had evaded their duty to fight. In Hitler's mind, Jews by their very nature were shirkers: people who refused to sacrifice their lives for a national community.

On June 22, 1941, Germany invaded the Soviet Union with 3 million troops. Hitler declared that this would be a "war of annihilation." In late 1941—as German and Soviet soldiers were dying in vast numbers—Hitler initiated the Final Solution. The Holocaust began—not in the gas chambers, but in the Soviet Union. Small groups of murderers—*Einsatzgruppen*—operated in the territories captured by German armies during the invasion. With the cooperation of the army, Jewish men, women and children were identified and massacred.

By mid-1942, approximately 1.5 million Jews had been killed in the Soviet Union. Hitler claimed to be undisturbed by the murder of men, women and children, declaring (Meltzer, 1976):

> If I don't mind sending the pick of the German people into the hell of war without the slightest regret over the spilling of precious German blood, then I naturally also have the right to eliminate millions of an inferior race that multiplies like vermin.

Genocide grew out of Hitler's thinking about warfare. Hitler knew that—as commander-in-chief of the army—he was permitted to send German soldiers to die in battle. Indeed, Hitler claims he doesn't mind "sending the pick of the German people into the hell of war" and doesn't have the slightest regret over the "spilling of precious German blood."

If Hitler had the right to send his own soldiers into the hell of war, why would he not also have the right to send Jews—an "inferior race that multiplies like vermin"—to their deaths? If he had no regrets about spilling precious German blood, why then should Hitler regret or feel guilty about the shedding of inferior Jewish blood?

Historian Ronald Hayman (1997) provides a report of an encounter between Hitler and his friend Henny von Schirach—who had returned to Germany from occupied Amsterdam in 1943 after she had become aware that helpless women were being transported to concentration camps. After dinner, Hitler turned to his friend: "You've come from Holland?" "Yes," she said, "That's why I'm here; I wanted talk to you. I've seen frightful things. I can't believe that's what you want."

Hitler said: "You're sentimental, Frau von Schirach." Then he jumped to his feet and formed two bowls with his hands. He moved his hands up and down like scales, declaring loudly and insistently:

Look—every day ten-thousands of my most valuable men are killed—men who are irreplaceable, the best. The balance is wrong; the equilibrium in Europe has been upset. Because the others aren't being killed. They survive—the ones in camps—the inferior ones. So what's it going to look like in Europe in a hundred years? In a thousand?

What would the world of the future be like if the most valuable people died while inferior people survived? Since German soldiers were dying, Jews would have to die too—to balance the scales of death.

CONCLUSION

True to words spoken before the war, Hitler did not hesitate to send millions of German soldiers to battle—where they were slaughtered. True to their oaths of allegiance, German soldiers honored their vows. They were obedient unto death. Insisting that the German people would never surrender, Hitler continued the war that he initiated right until he committed suicide on April 30, 1945. He fought on until the bitter end—even though by early 1943 military leaders realized that the war had been lost.

Over 4 million German soldiers were killed, many of them in the last year of the war when the situation was hopeless. Michael Geyer (2002) reports that more German soldiers were killed in action during the last year of the war than in the entire previous five years. During the last month of the war—told that 15,000 German officers had died in a futile attempt to defend Berlin—Hitler declared: "But that's what young men are for!"

Nazi genocide—the killing of mental patients and Jews—grew out of Hitler's understanding of the logic of warfare: his recognition that national leaders have the right to sacrifice—kill—their own soldiers. Nazi genocide proceeded based on the following reasoning: "If

Germany has the right to sacrifice (kill) its most valuable members—its soldiers—then certainly it also has the right to sacrifice (kill) its least valuable members—mental patients and Jews."

Victims of the Holocaust—like German soldiers—were required to submit absolutely to Germany. The Holocaust came into being according to the logic: If Germany can require that its soldiers be obedient unto death, Germany also can require that Jews be obedient unto death.

Hitler imagined that during the First World War, Jews had been shirkers—people who refused to sacrifice their lives for the community. Hitler decided that he would not permit a recurrence of this situation in the Second World War. Jews would not be allowed to get off scot-free. This time, they too would forfeit their lives.

Upon the death of a German soldier in the Second World War, newspapers carried the obituaries or farewells of men killed in action (Sorge, 1986). These announcements provided the name of the soldier, stating that the husband, father, brother, or uncle had died "For the Fuehrer, the German people and the fatherland." The Holocaust victim also died for Fuehrer and fatherland. The Holocaust enacted a perverted, degraded version of dying for the country—sacrificial death at the hands of the nation-state stripped of words like honor, heroism and glory.

BIBLIOGRAPHY

Aronsfeld, Caesar C. (1985). *The Text of the Holocaust: A Study of the Nazis' Extermination Propaganda, 1919-1945.* Marblehead, MA: Micah Publications.

Aronson, Ronald (1983). *Dialectics of Disaster: A Preface to Hope.* New York: Verso Books.

Audoin-Rouzeau, Stéphane (1992). *Men at War 1914-1918: National Sentiment and Trench Journalism in France During the First World War.* Oxford: Berg Publishing.

Baird, Jay W. (1974). *The Mythical World of Nazi War Propaganda, 1939-1945.* Minneapolis: University of Minnesota Press.

Barrès, Maurice (1918a). *The Faith of France: Studies in Spiritual Differences and Unity.* New York: Houghton Mifflin Company.

Barrès, Maurice (1918b). *The Undying Spirit of France.* New York: Houghton Mifflin Company.

Baynes, Norman H. (1942). *The Speeches of Adolf Hitler, April 1922–August 1939.* Two Volumes. New York: Oxford University Press.

Binding, Karl & Hoche, Alfred (1920). *Permission for the Destruction of Life Unworthy of Life.* Leipzig: Verlag von Felix Meiner.

Blackburn, Gil W. (1984). *Education in the Third Reich: A Study of Race and History in Nazi Textbooks.* New York: State University of New York Press.

Bourke, Joanna. (1996). *Dismembering the Male: Men's Bodies, Britain, and the Great War.* Chicago: University of Chicago Press.

Brundage, Burr Cartwright (1986). *The Jade Steps: A Ritual Life of the Aztecs.* Salt Lake City: University of Utah Press.

Coetzee, Frans. & Shevin-Coetzee, Marilyn. (1995). *Authority, Identity and the Social History of the Great War*. New York: Berghahn Books.

Dawson, Coningsby (1917). *Carry On: Letters in War-Time*. New York: John Lane Company.

Dawson, Coningsby (1918). *The Glory of the Trenches: An Interpretation*. New York: John Lane Company.

De Groot, Gerald (1988). *Douglas Haig: 1861-1928*. London: Unwin Hyman.

De Roussy de Sales, Raoul (1941). *My New Order*. New York: Reynal and Hitchcock.

Dyer, Gwynne (1985). *War*. New York: Crown Publishers.

Eksteins, Modris (1989). *Rites of Spring: The Great War and the Birth of the Modern Age*. New York: Anchor Books.

Elshtain, Jean Bethke (1987). *Women and War*. New York: Basic Books.

Feder, Gottfried (1971). *Hitler's Official Programme and Its Fundamental Ideas*. New York: Howard Fertig.

Fornari, Franco (1975). *The Psychoanalysis of War*. Bloomington: Indiana University Press.

Frank, Walter S. (2004). Adolf Hitler, The Making of a Fuhrer. *Smoter*. Retrieved August 22, 2008, from http://smoter.com/

Fritz, Stephen (1997). *Frontsoldaten: The German Soldier in World War II*. Lexington: University Press of Kentucky.

Genthe, Charles V. (1969). *American War Narratives 1917-1918: A Study and Bibliography*. New York: David Lews.

Geyer, Michael. (2002). 'There is a Land Where Everything is Pure: Its Name is Land of Death': Some Observations on Catastrophic Nationalism. In Greg Eghigan, ed. *Sacrifice and National Belonging*. Arlington: Texas University Press.

Gilbert, Martin (1994). *The First World War: A Complete History*. New York: Henry Holt and Company.

Gray, J. Glenn (1998). *The Warriors: Reflections on Men in Battle*. Lincoln, NE: Bison Books.

Haste, Cate (1977). *Keep the Home Fires Burning: Propaganda in the First World War.* London: Allen Lane.

Hayman, Ronald (1997). *Hitler and Geli.* New York: Bloomsburg.

Hellman, P. (1981). *Auschwitz Album.* New York: Random House.

Hitler, Adolf (1962). *Mein Kampf.* Boston: Houghton Mifflin Company.

Holt, John B. (1936). *Under the Swastika.* Chapel Hill: University of North Carolina Press.

Keegan, John (1976). *The Face of Battle.* New York: The Viking Press.

Kerr, Douglas (1993). *Wilfred Owen's Voice: Language and Community.* New York: Oxford University Press.

Koenigsberg, Richard A. (1975). *Hitler's Ideology: A Study in Psychoanalytic Sociology.* New York: The Library of Social Science.

Kubrick, Stanley. (Director) (1957). *Paths of Glory* [Motion picture]. Los Angeles: Metro-Goldwyn-Mayer Inc.

Kull, Steven (1984). "War as a Species Disorder." *Journal of Humanistic Psychology,* 24(3), 55-64.

Levi, Primo (1986). *The Drowned and the Saved.* New York: Summit Books.

Lifton, Robert J. (1986). *The Nazi Doctors: Medical Killing and the Psychology of Genocide.* New York: Basic Books.

Martin, Francis X. (1973). The Evolution of a Myth—The Easter Rising, Dublin 1916. In Eugene Kamenka, ed. *Nationalism: The Nature and Evolution of an Idea.* Canberra: Australian National University Press.

Marvin, Carolyn & Ingle, David W. (1999). *Blood Sacrifice and the Nation: Totem Rituals and the American Flag.* New York: Cambridge University Press.

Meltzer, Milton (1976). *Never to Forget: The Jews of the Holocaust.* New York: Harper & Row.

Miller, Steven E., Lynn-Jones, Sean M. & Van Evera, Stephen (1991). *Military Strategies and the Origins of the First World War.* Princeton: Princeton University Press.

Moctezuma, Eduardo M. (1995). *Life and Death in the Templo Mayor.* Niwot, Colorado: University Press of Colorado.

Murphy, Raymond E. et al. (1943). *"National Socialism." Basic Principles, Their Application by the Nazi Party's Foreign Organization, and the Use of Germans Abroad for Nazi Aims.* Washington: U.S. Department of State.

Noakes, Jeremy & Pridham, Geoffrey, Eds. (2001). *Nazism 1919-1945, Volume 3: Foreign Policy, War and Racial Extermination: A Documentary Reader.* Exeter: University of Exeter Press.

Padfield, Peter (1990). *Himmler: Reichsführer-SS.* New York: Henry Holt and Company.

Poliakov, Leon (1979). *Harvest of Hate: The Nazi Program for the Destruction of the Jews of Europe.* New York: Holocaust Library.

Proctor, Robert (1988). *Racial Hygiene: Medicine Under the Nazis.* Cambridge: Harvard University Press.

Rauschning, Hermann (1940). *The Voice of Destruction.* New York: G. P. Putnam's Sons.

Rhodes, James M. (1980). *The Hitler Movement: A Modern Millenarian Revolution.* Stanford: Hoover Institution Press.

Rubenfeld, Sheldon (2006). Healing by Killing: Medicine in the Third Reich. *Medicine Magazine.* Retrieved August 22, 2008, from http://www.medicinemagazine.us/

Scarry, Elaine (1987). *The Body in Pain: The Making and Unmaking of the World.* New York: Oxford University Press.

Snyder, Louis L. (1961). *Hitler and Nazism.* New York: Franklin Watts, Inc.

Sorge, Martin K. (1986). *The Other Price of Hitler's War: German Military and Civilian Losses Resulting from World War II.* Westport: Greenwood Press.

Soustell, Jacques (1970). *Daily Life of the Aztecs on the Eve of the Spanish Conquest.* Stanford: Stanford University Press.

Terraine, John (1982). *White Heat: The New Warfare 1914-18.* London: Sidgwick and Jackson.

Travers, Tim (1987). *The Killing Ground*. Boston: Allen and Unwin.

Weinreich, Max (1991). *Hitler's Professors: The Part of Scholarship in Germany's Crimes Against the Jewish People*. New Haven: Yale University Press.

Whalen, Robert W. (1984). *Bitter Wounds: German Victims of the Great War: 1914-1939*. Ithaca: Cornell University Press.

Winter, Denis (1979). *Death's Men: Soldiers of the Great War*. Great Britain: Penguin Books.

Winter, Jay (1996). *The Great War and the Shaping of the 20th Century* [Motion picture]. Alexandria, VA: PBS Home Video.

Wistrich, Robert S. (1985). *Hitler and the Holocaust*. New York: Random House.